Discovering
LOST RAILWAYS

F. G. Cockman

Shire Publications Ltd.

CONTENTS

Copyright © 1973 and 1988 by F. G. Cockman. First published 1973. Second edition 1976. Third edition 1980. Fourth edition 1985. Fifth edition 1988. Number 178 in the 'Discovering' series. ISBN 0 85263 916 3.

British Library Cataloguing in Publication data available.

Printed in Great Britain by C. I. Thomas & Sons (Haverfordwest) Ltd.

PREFACE

In 1939 our railways had reached the peak of efficiency for steam and because of this they were able to help Britain win the war far more than the roads. But they wore themselves out in so doing. It was obvious after the war that private finance could never fully restore, let alone impove, the railway system, and so nationalisation was inevitable. The 1947 Act did not, strangely enough, integrate the railways in a national transport system but continued to segregate them as they were when privately owned, and laid upon them the burden of paying 3 per cent per annum on the new Transport stock. Nevertheless BR made a profit from 1948 to 1954 inclusive. Space does not permit an examination of the causes of the gradual loss of 'profitability' but the remedy of closing hundreds of branch lines was quite unsound.

The purpose of this book is to describe certain interesting routes of former railway lines, but it in no way implies that access may be had to these routes as a matter of right. Before entering on to any such premises which are not clearly designated as a public footway, members of the public should inquire as to what, if any, permission is required and obtain the necessary consent.

For the fourth edition, I have revisited most of the railways and amended the text. As a general rule, where the old track bed is on an embankment or at ground level walking is still practicable. In cuttings, however, the accumulation of rain water has encouraged trees, bushes and weeds.

It only remains for me to acknowledge the great help I received in writing this book. In the course of discovering lost railways one must unfortunately travel many miles by car and I could never have found my way across country to reach the deserted stations without the skilful map-reading of Frances, my wife. I owe much to my friends John J. Davis and C. W. Collard for their invaluable help with the photographs, and last, but certainly not least, I must express my appreciation for the assistance I have had from the staff at the Public Record Office, always so cheerfully given.

Bedford   F. G. COCKMAN

The cover picture shows Class 9 2-10-0 No 92033 on an up freight train passing Braunston and Willoughby in 1964. The station was closed on 1st April 1957.

On the maps in this book the lost railways are indicated by broken lines, and the principal stations on them are shown in capitals. Other railways are denoted by heavy, crossed lines and main roads by light, unbroken lines.

1. HALWILL JUNCTION TO PADSTOW

Acts: various by the L&SWR. Opened: Bodmin to Wade-bridge (independent), 4th July 1834 (to L & SWR 1845); Oke-hampton to Lydford, October 1874; Meldon to Holsworthy, 20th January 1879; Halwill to Launceston, 21st July 1886; Launceston to Wadebridge, 1st June 1895; Wadebridge to Padstow, 27th March 1899. Closed: Halwill to Wadebridge, 3rd October 1966; Bodmin to Padstow, 30th January 1967. Length 49¾ miles.

One of the surprising things about the gradual extension of the London & South Western Railway from Salisbury to the far west is that it appeared to be unnoticed by the broad-gauge hierarchy. This was partly due to the fact that relations between the Great Western and the Bristol & Exeter railways were sometimes strained and the growth of the standard-gauge line failed to attract attention. After reaching Salisbury on 1st May 1857 the South Western pushed on to Exeter (Queen Street) where the station was first used on 19th July 1860. As early as 1845 the board of the L&SWR had purchased the little Bodmin & Wadebridge Railway, and two years later they gained control of the Exeter & Crediton line. These were to act as stepping stones to the west and when the Okehampton Railway was absorbed a rapid movement into Cornwall resulted as shown above. The line ran through difficult country for the engineer, but most attractive to the tourist, and the gradients were severe with many curves of short radius. From Halwill to Launceston there were no exceptional engineering works but at the latter place three rivers, the Kensey, the Tamar and the Carey, had to be bridged. Egloskerry station was 362 feet above sea level, and Tresmeer 558, giving a climb at an average gradient of 1 in 94. Deep cuttings beyond Otterham led to the summit near the village of Halwill Barton, and beyond Camelford where the station was about one mile from the town, there was a steady fall from 758 feet to 261 feet above sea level at St Kew Highway station—an average of 1 in 90. Near Wadebridge the line crossed the rivers Allen and Camel. In the first year of the opening the L&SWR ran six trains each way between Halwill and Padstow, but none on Sundays, and these were reduced to four by 1920 although two of them, the 10.00 and the 13.00 from Waterloo, had luncheon cars. Under British Rail there were two through trains daily from Padstow to London and two in the reverse direction,

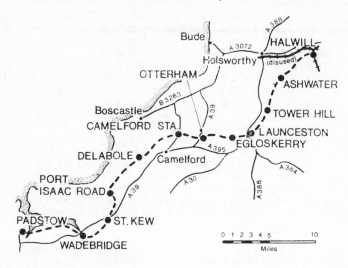

with another two each way between Halwill and Padstow. The Padstow-Bodmin line had five in each direction weekdays only. There never were Sunday trains. The last 'ACE' ran from London to Padstow on 5th September 1964 behind No. 34015 *Exmouth.*

Among the early engines on this line were the Beattie 2-4-0Ts, built in 1874, and fortunately two are now being restored — No 30587 by the Dart Valley Railway and No 0314 by the Buckinghamshire Railway Centre, but the best engines for local work were Maunsell's N Class 2-6-0s (plate 1).

Halwill was once a busy junction (plate 1) but now the station is demolished and the platforms overgrown. The surface soon improves with a grassy walk to **Ashwater** with the station name boards still to be seen. The house is privately occupied and the space between the platforms filled in. Next comes **Tower Hill,** with a familiar London ring as if an electric Circle train would appear. There are, however, only platforms to be seen and the visitor can push on to **Launceston.** Here, it is disappointing to find that the once pretty station (plate 2) has disappeared with factory buildings covering the site, but the historic castle and church provide some compensation. We have now entered Cornwall and the old line ran through some very attractive country to **Egloskerry.** Here again the

5

house is used as a residence with a garden full of flowers where the trains used to run. The name of the station is still displayed. The same remarks can be applied to the next station—**Tresmeer**. There is little to see at **Otterham** but **Camelford** station is worth a visit because the buildings, now used for storage, are in good condition. This station suffered from being distant from the town. **Delabole** may well be missed as the nearby quarry is rather depressing but he who persists will be rewarded with a delightful walk past **Port Isaac Road** to **St Kew Highway**. The track bed is soft and grassy and the sides of the deep cuttings abound in wild flowers. Go in April and you will be gladdened by the sight of so many primroses and wild violets. At St Kew the widening of the main road has blotted out much of the track, but the station house is now a guest house with a most attractive garden. The line ends with a good view of the river Camel. **Wadebridge** station is now known as the John Betjeman Centre with a library and workshops. And so to **Padstow**—one of the pleasantest towns in the Duchy. Padstow station is now occupied as offices by Padstow Town Council. The three span girder bridge is now used as a footpath. This was a grand line to travel on and the visitor today will find his trip rewarding.

Train: Bodmin Parkway is the most convenient station.

Car: The most useful roads are A30, A39 and A388.

2. SIDMOUTH JUNCTION TO SIDMOUTH AND EXMOUTH

Sidmouth Junction to Sidmouth: act 1871, opened 6th July 1874; Tipton St John to Budleigh Salterton: act 1894, opened 15th May 1897. Budleigh Salterton to Exmouth: act 1898, opened 1st June 1903. Sidmouth Junction to Sidmouth (8¼ miles); closed 6th March 1967. Tipton St John to Exmouth (11¼ miles); closed 6th March 1967.

Anyone discovering lost railways in this pretty countryside will find that he is walking over the tracks of three separate concerns. The L&SWR main line to Exeter had been open only two years when a scheme was evolved to join Sidmouth to it by rail, but by 1865 the plans had evaporated. After an

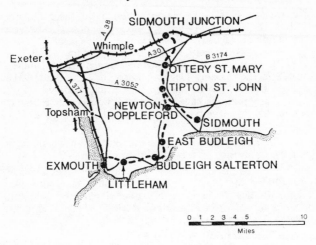

interval of six years the promoters were successful and a branch was duly opened serving also Ottery St Mary and Tipton St John (plate 3). It was unfortunate that the station at Sidmouth Junction served nowhere in particular and that Sidmouth station was about one mile from the sea. Over twenty years passed before another company built the line from Tipton to Budleigh Salterton, and finally the L&SWR stepped in and joined Budleigh to Exmouth. They took over the line from Tipton to Budleigh in 1911 but the Sidmouth branch remained independent until absorbed by the Southern Railway in 1923. For the most part the gradients are easy as the line followed the course of the river Otter.

At the turn of the century Sidmouth enjoyed a service of nine trains daily (except Sundays) to and from Sidmouth Junction. A similar number ran between Tipton and Exmouth. The last days of the L&SWR saw the services reduced to seven in each direction, Sundays excepted, but with refreshment car trains available from Waterloo to Sidmouth Junction at 11.00, 13.00 and 15.00. The 10.38 and 12.26 from Sidmouth Junction to London gave similar facilities. In the 1960s British Rail had increased the Sidmouth services to thirteen trains to and from the junction, with two on Sundays. Although the Tipton-Exmouth line still had no Sunday service, the weekday trains had increased to ten each way. In addition through carriages were attached to the 11.00 from Waterloo for Sidmouth and to the 10.20 from Sidmouth.

7

Various types of tank engine appeared on these branches including the Adams 0-4-4 and 4-4-2 designs. In later years Drummond's sturdy M7 0-4-4s did the work (plate 3).

The best walk is from **Ottery St Mary,** where there is an interesting church, through **Newton Poppleford** to **Budleigh Salterton** in the pleasing Devon countryside. The old trackbed is mostly grassed over as are the station platforms which still remain. The buildings have largely disappeared and **Sidmouth Junction,** like its neighbour Seaton Junction, is a ghost of its former self.

Train: The nearest station is now Exmouth from which exploration can commence by way of Littleham.

Bus: Devon General services are plentiful (Nos 380/381 Exeter-Ottery St. Mary, 382 Exeter-Tipton St. Johns, X57 Exmouth-Budleigh Salterton-Newton Poppleford-Sidmouth, 339 Sidmouth-Newton Poppleford-Exeter, 341/342 Sidmouth-Ottery St. Mary, 330/331 Exmouth-Littleham).

Car: The roads are A30, A35 and A377.

3. DEVON & SOMERSET RAILWAY

Act: 29th July 1864. Opened: Norton Fitzwarren to Wiveliscombe, 8th June 1871; Wiveliscombe to Barnstaple, 1st November 1873. Length: 42¾ miles. Closed: 3rd October 1966.

As first constructed this railway was single throughout with a gauge of 7ft 0¼in. For the first three years the Bristol & Exeter Railway supplied locomotives and coaching stock, but in 1876 the GWR became responsible for working the line which they took over completely on 1st July 1901. The route lay through beautiful country but the engineering work was heavy, added to which the financial crisis of 1866 imposed some economy in construction. The line climbed at 1 in 66 and 1 in 70 between Norton Fitzwarren and Milverton. Bathealton Tunnel, between Wiveliscombe and Venn Cross stations, was 447 yards long and was approached at a gradient of 1 in 58. There was a very fine viaduct, 101 feet high, which carried the rails over the river Tone near Venn Cross. Proceeding westwards, locomotives had to negotiate a climb at 1 in 58 once again to reach the summit near East Anstey, after which their work was easier. Before reaching Filleigh station the line crossed the river Bray on a viaduct 232 yards long and 94 feet high, succeeded by Castle Hill Tunnel which had a length of 321 yards. After 1868 all GWR branches were altered to

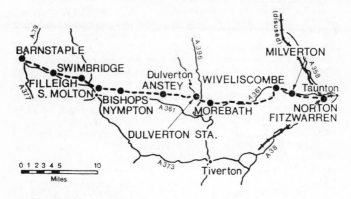

standard gauge, and this work was carried out on the Devon & Somerset in 1881. A connection was made with the L&SWR at Barnstaple in 1887.

A service of six trains in each direction between Taunton and Barnstaple was provided on weekdays in 1873, Sundays having two only. Fifty years later the number of trains was the same and there was a coach slipped at Taunton off the 12 noon express from Paddington which connected with the 15.10 to Barnstaple. In 1956 the 13.20 from Barnstaple made a connection with the up 'Bristolian', thus giving a very fast journey to Paddington. By 1966 there were five trains each way on the branch, weekdays only, and the line was suffering from the fact that most of the stations were not very near the towns they served. After 1881 the GWR sent their various types of 4-4-0 to work the branch, and in later years the very useful 2-6-0s of the 43xx class handled the traffic most competently (plate 4).

For some reason the ballast has not been removed from the track of this line so that walking is a little more uncomfortable and rubber boots are advisable. **Norton Fitzwarren** station has gone but two rusty tracks still curve away to the north-west, the right-hand one going to Minehead, awaiting possible purchase, and the left, the former Devon & Somerset Railway, extending only a few hundred yards. At **Milverton** the station site is a traffic roundabout, and towards **Wiveliscombe** the embankments and cuttings succeed each other past orchards and green hilly country. This is another line which is best

9

seen in the spring because of its wild flowers. Just before Wiveliscombe road widening has destroyed the old formation but the station buildings stand and are used for storage, with the space between the platforms filled with earth. The fine viaduct over the river Tone has lost its steel girders and only the stone piers remain. However, the track can be followed again just east of Bathealton Tunnel, which is straight and dry and safe for walking. Immediately west of the tunnel is **Venn Cross** station where only the goods sheds are to be seen. Along the track a discarded chair tells its own story—'BR(W)1957GKN95'. At **Morebath** the station house has been prettily redecorated and is called Primrose Cottage, while at **Dulverton** the station buildings are part of the Caernarvon Arms Hotel. Some of the track hereabouts is grassed over and makes walking easy. **East Anstey** station is in private occupation and between here and Bishops Nympton several underline bridges have been removed. These gaps cause little difficulty. Some portions of the line have been sold to neighbouring farmers who use the station buildings as stores. **Bishops Nympton** is one of these. Proceeding to **South Molton** (plate 4) we find the station now used as offices, and further on the walk has to be interrupted as the viaduct over the river Bray has met the same fate as that over the Tone. Next comes Castle Hill Tunnel, also suitable for exploration, and its width reminds one that broad-gauge engines used to run through it. Just before **Filleigh** the track is blocked by a large earth tip. The station buildings are privately occupied and are of sombre stone, relieved in April by a host of golden daffodils. Thence on to Swimbridge past quiet and beautiful woods maintained by the Forestry Commission. At **Swimbridge** the buildings have disappeared and there is nothing to delay the visitor who can now set out for **Barnstaple.** Here the GWR Victoria Road station was closed on 13th June 1960 and trains were diverted to the junction. The town has a very fine church.

Train: To Taunton or Barnstaple.

Bus: Western National services 205 Taunton-Milverton-Wiveliscombe, 307 and 359 Barnstaple-South Molton. Terraneau's buses run from South Molton to Dulverton.

Car: Take the road A361.

4. SOMERSET & DORSET JOINT RAILWAY

Somerset Central Railway: act 17th June 1852, opened 28th August 1854. Dorset Central Railway: act 29th July 1856, opened 31st October 1860. Bath to Bournemouth West (71½ miles); closed 5th March 1966. Evercreech Junction to Burnham (24¼ miles); closed 29th October 1951. Glastonbury to Wells (5½ miles); closed 29th October 1951. Edington Junction to Bridgwater (7¾ miles); closed 1st December 1952. (Total mileage 108½).

The traveller who has made the rail journey from Bath to Bournemouth will carry with him memories of a splendid line running through delightful scenery and the sound of locomotives hard at work. The Somerset & Dorset began as the two separate companies referred to above. The Somerset Central was laid to the broad gauge and ran from Highbridge to Glastonbury, being extended to Bruton (Cole) on 3rd February 1862. The southern partner was built to standard gauge and the first section lay between Wimborne and Blandford. The next year saw Cole and Templecombe linked by rail and the two companies joined commercially but not physically on 7th June 1862 to become the Somerset & Dorset Railway. The missing link, from Templecombe to Blandford was opened on 31st August 1863, and as by now the Somerset section had been laid with a third rail, trains could run from Wimborne to Highbridge. By 1870 the S&DR had rid itself of all traces of the broad gauge. The extension from Evercreech Junction to Bath was authorised in 1871 and the first train ran on 20th July 1874. Two years later the Midland and the L&SWR leased the line for 999 years and these companies worked the first train on the Edington to Bridgwater branch on 21st July 1890.

The northern half of the line traverses the Mendip Hills and it is here that the engineering works were the most expensive and the gradients the most formidable. For example, immediately after leaving Bath Junction (the real starting point of the Somerset & Dorset) the line climbs at 1 in 50 through Devonshire Tunnel. There is a fall at 1 in 103 after leaving Combe Down Tunnel to Midford where there is a viaduct 168 yards long. After Radstock the ascent over the Mendips begins in earnest, the engines having to face a haul of about 2¾ miles at 1 in 50 through Midsomer Norton to the tunnel before Chilcompton. The summit is between Binegar and Masbury after which there is a drop at 1 in 50 for nearly three miles through Winsor Hill Tunnel to Shepton Mallet. The railway here is at a high level with imposing viaducts known as the Charlton and the Bath Road. The former is 317 yards long. After Evercreech Junction the going is much easier until Broadstone where there is a climb at 1 in 80 and a drop at 1 in 75, both about two miles in extent. The next 7½ miles to Bournemouth West present no difficulty. The Burnham branch was much easier, seven miles being level.

When the L&SWR opened the Broadstone and Poole branch on 2nd December 1872 the S&D abandoned the service to Wimborne and commenced running their trains into Bournemouth West, thus fulfilling their ambition of 'joining coast to coast'. It was about this time that they became owners of steamships and thus could convey passengers from Cardiff to Bournemouth via Highbridge. This venture was not, however, successful and only added to the company's financial difficulties.

In 1875 the company provided a service of five trains each way on weekdays between Bath and Bournemouth West, but there was none on Sundays. There were, of course, local trains covering shorter journeys. In 1920 seven trains ran from Bournemouth West to Bath and six in the opposite direction, but still none on Sundays. At this time the 14.45 train from Bath to Bournemouth West came through from Derby with a restaurant car. The 9.35 from Bournemouth West to Derby also had this facility. In later years the famous 'Pines Express' cut the journey time but on 8th September 1962 it ran for the last time over this route and thereafter passed through Oxford, Reading and Basingstoke. Another blow to the S&D was the closure of Bournemouth West station on 14th June 1965, followed on 5th March 1966 by the demise of the whole system.

Long stretches of the railway consisted of single track—Bath Junction to Midford, Templecombe to Blandford and Corfe Mullen Junction to Broadstone. The whole of the Burnham branch was single-line. This type of railway requires careful management if accidents are to be avoided and unfortunately there was a bad collision near Radstock on 7th August 1876, caused by negligence. An excursion train going north met an empty stock train running south. This was just after the MR and L&SWR had taken over and before they had had time to effect improvements. Thereafter the railway was brought up to a high standard and enjoyed a good record for safety. Two other accidents, less serious, may be mentioned.

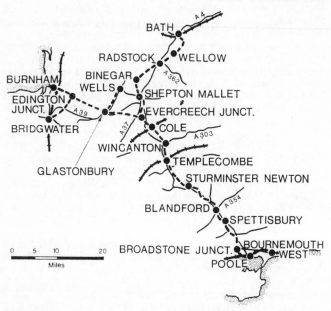

On 20th November 1929 a goods train ran out of control down the 1 in 50 to Bath Junction and was wrecked, and on 29th July 1936 an 0-6-0T engine ran away unmanned from Radstock to near the same place where it was derailed.

The locomotives had a distinctly Derby flavour and for many years resembled Midland 0-6-0s, 4-4-0s, 0-4-4Ts and 0-6-0Ts. The most famous were the eleven Fowler 2-8-0s which appeared new from Derby in 1914. Both in the 1914 and the 1939 wars Southern T9 4-4-0s took their turn, and in later years the Bulleid 'West Country' class hauled the expresses although they needed Midland class 2 4-4-0s as pilots if the loads were heavy. In the last months BR standard class 5 4-6-0s were very happy with four coaches, while the class 9 2-10-0s (plate 6) dealt with heavy trains in their usual competent fashion.

As **Bath (Green Park)** station is now Sainsburys the visit is best commenced at Bath Junction which was the real beginning of the S&DJR. The track bed thence to Devonshire Tunnel is now a public footpath and it is recommended that the walk be resumed after the next tunnel, known as Combe

13

Down. **Midford** station is privately occupied and **Shoscombe** halt demolished (the surrounding site is private). It was on this curvy stretch of line that one could sit in a coach near the end of the train and watch the engines pulling hard. It may come as a surprise to the visitor after several miles of green agricultural countryside to find himself entering the industrial belt of Somerset. From Writhlington to Midsomer Norton he will see the slag heaps of the West Country coal mines. In the centre of this district stood **Radstock North** station, but now it has gone. The Somerset & Dorset Circle has been replaced by the Somerset & Dorset Railway Museum Trust, with its headquarters on the West Somerset Railway at Washford. Here work is continuing on the S&DJR 2-8-0 locomotive No 53808, one of a batch built specially at Derby for working on the S&DJR. See Appendix for further details. There are also passenger coaches and goods stock, some of which were used in the film *Young Winston*. After leaving Radstock one heads for **Chilcompton** and **Binegar,** high up in open country. There is little left of either of these stations. The summit of the Mendips is passed at **Masbury** whence the line descends to **Shepton Mallet**. The surface is quite good.

Although this station is now in ruins the great viaducts to the north and the south are still there to be admired. A pleasant walk takes one to **Evercreech (New)** which is gradually being obliterated by a new housing estate. Further south, near **Evercreech Junction,** the viaduct over the meadows of the river Alham remains and level-crossing gates mark where the railway crossed road A371. The GWR main line to Taunton is crossed over just before **Cole,** and you can then walk on to **Wincanton** station where the stone buildings are intact but the track bed has been filled in up to platform level. The once important junction of **Templecombe** has now vanished although British Rail reopened the station here in 1983. The site of the engine sheds, where 53808 could often be seen, is now covered with factory buildings, and here the S&DJR burrowed under the L&SWR to reach **Henstridge**. After this station the county boundary is crossed and we enter Dorset. This part of the walk is through the lovely Blackmore Vale and we pass on to **Stalbridge** where only the level-crossing gates enable one to identify the site. At **Sturminster Newton** the goods sheds and platforms mark the spot, and the walk from there to **Shillingstone** along the picturesque Stour valley is something not to be missed. Shillingstone station is intact and it brings to mind memories of many journeys over this wonderful line. And so to **Blandford Forum** (plate 6) where the substantial station buildings have now unfortunately been demolished. There is a short viaduct just south of the station, and a pause can be made here to view the splendid church of Saints Peter and Paul. The track can now be followed to **Bailey Gate** and **Broadstone,** which was once such an important junction, but Broadstone to Poole is now an industrial estate and inaccessible.

From **Glastonbury** the line may be traced to **Wells** where there is little left of the station. You cannot leave Wells, however, without looking over the cathedral or its rival in architecture—St Cuthbert's church. There is also a pleasant walk along the original line of the Somerset Central to **Highbridge** (plate 5), although the terrain, alongside Tadham Moor, is flat. At **Edington Junction** the station buildings are private but you can still see the level-crossing gates and the Railway Inn. The later branch to **Bridgwater** is worth following if only to visit **Cossington** station (private) and the nearby village, one of the prettiest in Somerset.

Train: To Bath (Spa), Highbridge and Bridgwater.

Bus: Bristol Omnibus Co. services—Bath to Midford 178, 254; Bath to Wellow and Shoscombe 178; Bath to Radstock and Midsomer Norton 177, 184, 175, 176, 365, 366, 368; Radstock to Chilcompton 178; Radstock to Shepton Mallet 176; Radstock to Binegar 175; Bath to Wells 175; Shepton Mallet to Evercreech 265; Bristol to Highbridge and Burnham 369; Weston-super-Mare to Highbridge and Burnham 132, 133, 134, 135, 138 and 139; Bristol to Radstock and Frome 365, 367; Wells to Glastonbury 165, 167, 376. Western National—Yeovil to Henstridge and Wincanton 468. Hants. & Dorset—Bournemouth to Broadstone, 10, 10A, 22; Bournemouth, Spettisbury and Blandford, 24, 24B; Poole to Broadstone 30, 30A.

Car: roads A357 and A371.

5. MID-WALES RAILWAY

Act: 1st August 1859. Opened: 21st September 1864. Length (Moat Lane Junction to Talyllyn Junction): 56 miles. Closed: 31st December 1962.

The remote centre of Wales badly wanted improved communications by the middle of the nineteenth century and it needed a great deal of enthusiasm and money to lay down a railway. The Mid-Wales Railway had plenty of the former but was perpetually short of capital. The Llanidloes and Newtown Railway had opened for traffic on 2nd September 1859 and the Mid-Wales filled in the gap between Llanidloes and Talyllyn Junction, the latter being situated on the Brecon & Merthyr Railway dating from 1st May 1863. The Mid-Wales opened its line in three sections—Three Cocks Junction to Talyllyn, Llanidloes to Newbridge, and Newbridge to Three Cocks. A curve was put in to connect with the Central Wales Railway (L&NWR) on 1st November 1866. The Mid-Wales was a difficult line to work. Going south from Llanidloes there was a climb of nearly 6½ miles at 1 in 75 to Penpontbren Junction. Here the Manchester & Milford Railway had started building a branch to Aberystwyth but it had stopped short at Llangurig and only one train ever ran on it. Just beyond Tylwch a climb at 1 in 111 leads to the summit, 6¾ miles from Llanidloes, and the first tunnel is encountered at Marteg, 372 yards long and down at 1 in 90. This is 10½ miles from the start. The going was easier to Rhayader, and then came Rhayader tunnel (271 yards up at 1 in 75) after which there was a junction with the line serving the Elan Valley water works (Birmingham Corporation). The line fell at 1 in 60 to Doldowlod and so through Newbridge to Builth Road, which was at first called Llechryd, where the Central Wales line crossed above it. There followed a fall at 1 in 100 to Builth where the Mid-Wales had their locomotive and carriage works. At nearly 27 miles from Llanidloes the loco works was nearly half-way. After Aberedw there was a rise at 1 in 75 to Tyr Celyn, followed by a fall at 1 in 91 to Erwood. Gradients were easier to Trefeinon where the line rose at 1 in 75 to Talyllyn.

For the first two years contractors ran the trains, which were three each way over the whole length on weekdays, Sundays having only one train each way between Builth Wells and Llanidloes. In 1866 the company took over and maintained the services until 1888 when the Cambrian undertook the work. Just before the 1923 Grouping these services were unaltered except that the Sunday train ran the whole distance. Shortly before closure the Sunday trains had disappeared and there were only two weekday trains over the whole length, supplemented by two trains between Builth Wells and Moat Lane.

The Mid-Wales company owned six 0-4-2 and six 0-6-0 engines made by Kitson, and two 0-6-0s from Sharp Stewart. The Cambrian Railways used 2-4-0s and Herbert Jones's design

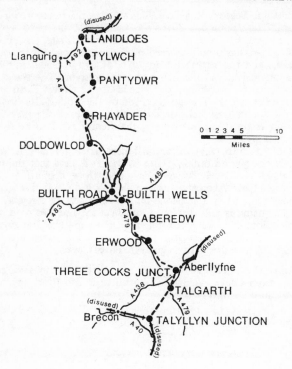

of 4-4-0. In GWR days the 0-4-2T appeared and under British Rail the useful standard class 2 Moguls handled the traffic, the numbers being between 46503 and 46524.

Llanidloes station buildings are demolished but walking is pleasant to Tylwch and Pantydwr, the station buildings at each place being in private occupation. At St Harmons station the level-crossing gates are in position but the track is covered with new bungalows. Exploration can next be continued to Rhayader where the Powys County Council has taken over the station buildings, which are therefore in good condition. Beyond Rhayader Tunnel was the junction for the Elan Valley reservoir. Although the site of the next station, **Doldowlod,** has been taken over for a caravan site, the railway atmosphere has been preserved by the maintenance of the name boards, and the setting up, in 1970, of two immaculate GWR semaphore signals, one home and one distant. The track bed is suitable for rambling past **Newbridge** to **Builth Road** (formerly Llechryd). The goods sheds of the Mid-Wales line are in use for commercial purposes and, of course, the high-level station is open as, fortunately, the Central Wales line is still functioning.

Going south, the visitor will next arrive at **Builth Wells** where the station buildings are in use. It is here that the walk is along the lovely Wye valley, and these delightful views continue past **Aberedw** (station demolished) and **Tir Celyn,** where there is a fine stone-built residence. At **Erwood** the station name is still displayed and here the line has been converted into a motor road for two miles towards **Boughrood.** The station has gone but the railway bridge over the Wye exists. Thence the going is good to **Three Cocks.**

Train: The enthusiast will wish to visit the line by taking the train from Craven Arms or Llanelli to Builth Road, and then to explore north and south.

Bus: Services are unfortunately scanty. The National Welsh service No 730 runs from Brecon to Hay.

Car: Motorists can use roads A483 and A470.

6. BEDFORD & CAMBRIDGE RAILWAY

Act: 6th August 1860. Opened: 1st August 1862. Length: 29¾ miles. Closed: 31st December 1967.

Soon after Robert Stephenson had surveyed the Bedford Railway (Bletchley to Bedford) in 1844, he was instructed to inspect the territory between Bedford and Cambridge with a view to the extension of the line. This he did in 1845 and his line would have taken the normal route across to Sandy after which it curved north-east to Tetworth and Waresley. The scheme was rejected in Standing Orders and abandoned,

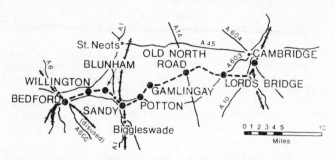

but the Bedford Railway was opened on 17th November 1846. Several other abortive schemes were projected but in the late 1850s William Henry Whitbread formed the Bedford & Cambridge Railway Company which duly obtained its act. About the same time a small private railway had been built and this was to play its part in the construction of the Bedford & Cambridge Railway. When, in 1850, the Great Northern Railway began to serve Sandy, Captain William Peel RN (a son of Sir Robert Peel), decided to build a line from his estate at Potton across the 3½ miles of country to effect a junction with the main line. Thus in 1857 the little Sandy & Potton Railway came into being and as it lay entirely on Captain Peel's land no act of Parliament was necessary. The Board of Trade duly approved the line for passenger carrying and the first train ran on 9th November 1857. The railway was operated on the basis of 'one engine in steam', the locomotive being an 0-4-0T made by George England at their Surrey works for £800. The firm later supplied a second engine known as *Little England*, also 0-4-0T. It is sad to have to record that such an enthusiast as Captain Peel never saw his railway. His ship was ordered to the Crimea where he served with distinction and was one of the first to be awarded the Victoria Cross. At the end of the war his frigate *Shannon* was among those which went to India to quell the Mutiny. Captain Peel survived the fighting but died of smallpox in India on 22nd April 1858. The Sandy & Potton Railway ran four trains each way on weekdays and none on Sundays. As the Bedford & Cambridge Railway progressed to the east it absorbed the Sandy & Potton, using its alignment, with resulting sharp curves and gradients of 1 in 100. After Gamlingay the line had to climb at 1 in 105 past Hayley Woods (now a nature reserve) and to descend to Old North Road at the same gradient. The rest of the line

19

is level or thereabouts. Of the stations opened in 1862 all were well placed except Gamlingay which was kept a mile from the town owing to the vigorous opposition of the Turnpike Trustees. When Old North Road station was built, the road was of greater importance than the Great North Road (A1) but its rival soon took the ascendancy after bridge widenings were made, such as at Tempsford. Lord's Bridge station was named after Lord Oxford, the lord of the manor who had constructed a bridge over the marshy land for the benefit of his tenants. The railway cannot lay claim to any tunnels or notable viaducts.

In 1862 there were five trains each way between Bedford and Cambridge (one on Sundays) and by 1922 one additional down train had been put on. In 1967, the last year, there were eight diesel trains in each direction, some stopping only at Sandy. There were no Sunday trains. Early locomotives were the Allan 'Crewe' 2-2-2s, followed by Ramsbottom or Webb 2-4-0s (some compounds). Later the line was a favourite haunt of the 'Prince of Wales' 4-6-0s, *Lusitania* being most frequently seen. Midland 4-4-0s (Class 2) then took over, with an infrequent compound, until the Stanier Black 5 and the 2-6-4Ts replaced them. Finally there were some BR Standard 2-6-4Ts and Class 4 4-6-0s which in turn gave way to the diesels.

The line had been worked by the London & North Western from the start and absorption took place in 1865. When Dr Beeching made his evaluation in 1963 he accepted the Bedford-Cambridge branch and it was the British Railways Board, which, under Government pressure, decided to withdraw services. Thus there is no east-west cross country link lying between London and the Birmingham-Leicester-Stamford route.

Between Bedford and Willington, the Anglian Water Authority has established a depot across the track bed and houses are built on the track each side of Sandy.

Up at Sandy the Royal Society for the Protection of Birds has extensive grounds worth visiting. After Gamlingay there is the Hayley Woods nature reserve, and the beauty of the city of Cambridge requires no elaboration here. **Willington** station (timber built) has been demolished and also **Sandy** (LNW), which is a pity as the latter's iron roof brackets containing the letters 'B-C' (Bedford-Cambridge) have disappeared. Happily these can still be seen at **Potton** where also Captain Peel's engine shed survives. The station buildings at **Blunham, Potton,**

Gamlingay and **Old North Road** (plates 7 and 8) have been sold for private occupation.

A few notes on the locomotive *Shannon* would not be out of place. After working on the Sandy & Potton Railway it was used in the construction of the line to Cambridge; then it was sent to Crewe for shunting purposes. For a time it appeared on the Cromford & High Peak Railway, and ended its working life on the Wantage Tramroad. This line closed in 1947 when the Western Region of BR restored the engine at Swindon. *Shannon* stood on Wantage Road station down platform until 1964 when the station was closed and the engine passed into the care of the Great Western Society who keep it at Didcot. It is well worth a trip there to see this veteran of over one and a quarter centuries in steam.

Two further points relating to the Bedford-Cambridge line should be mentioned. In 1887 the LNWR tested the new Tyer electric tablet system on the single line between Bedford and Sandy. In 1938 the LMS tested their new three-car diesel electric train between Oxford and Cambridge via Bedford. The service did not appear in the public timetables and it did not survive the war, but it pointed the way to the future.

Train: To explore the line one can go by train to Bedford and walk east.

Bus: Bedford — Blunham — Sandy — Potton — Gamlingay No 178. Bedford — Willington No 176. Bedford — Cambridge, coach services X1, X2 and X3.

Car: Motorists can choose from A6, A1 and A14 roads.

7. GREAT CENTRAL RAILWAY
(Nottingham to Quainton Road)

Act: 28th March 1893. Opened: 15th March 1899. Length: 82½ miles. Closed: some stations north of Aylesbury, 4th March 1963; Nottingham Victoria to Arkwright Street and Rugby to Calvert, 3rd September 1966; Arkwright Street to Rugby, 3rd May 1969.

One of the great railway promoters of the nineteenth century was Sir Edward Watkin and by the end of the 1880s he held the position of chairman of four railway companies—the Manchester Sheffield & Lincolnshire, the Metropolitan, the East

London and the South Eastern. It is understandable that he should wish to connect the first two by bridging the gap between Annesley and Quainton Road. This extension would provide a new route to London from Manchester, Sheffield, Nottingham, Leicester and Rugby and naturally it incurred the hostility of the London & North Western and the Midland Railways which already served those towns. The Great Northern also joined the opposition as Watkin proposed to ignore an agreement whereby the MS&L sent their Manchester trains to King's Cross via Retford. The opposition succeeded in having the 1892 Bill rejected but Watkin triumphed the next year. The engineer, Sir Douglas Fox, built a splendid main line with a maximum grade of 1 in 176 and mile after mile of track suitable for high-speed running. The work was expensive and the total cost of £6 million is partly accounted for by the excavations for Nottingham (Victoria) station with its two tunnels, one being 1,189 yards long. Also, in Northamptonshire the uplands had to be burrowed through near Catesby with a tunnel of 2,997 yards. There were viaducts at Whetstone (152 yards), Staverton (119 yards), Catesby (158 yards), and Helmdon (119 yards). The magnificent viaduct over the valley of the Great Ouse south of Brackley was no less than 252 yards. The last two miles into Marylebone were very costly in view of the long tunnels (partly under Lord's cricket ground) and because of the extensive demolition of property. In 1897 the MS&LR changed its name to 'Great Central'.

As the new main line failed to attract the heavy traffic hoped for, its trains were light and few in number, but very fast and punctual. To commence with there were twelve passenger trains daily between London and Nottingham and eleven in the reverse direction. On Sundays four trains ran each way. A good example of the kind of express running on the Great Central was the 18.20 from London which covered the 126½ miles to Nottingham in 135 minutes, slipping a coach at Leicester.

In 1900 the GCR benefited from two quite different events. One was the opening of the Woodford-Banbury line on 13th August, and the other was the appointment of J. G. Robinson as locomotive engineer. The Banbury branch was built with the financial help of the Great Western, it being a *quid pro quo* arising out of the abandonment by the GCR of their support for the projected London & South Wales Railway, which, if built, would have harmed the GWR.

With John Robinson as locomotive designer, the GCR came to possess some of the most beautiful engines ever to run in Britain. A further strengthening took place in 1902 with the arrival of Sam Fay as general manager. His genius soon made the GCR respected all over the country, not only because of the speed and punctuality of trains on his own system but also by virtue of running powers in all directions. For example, in 1920 there were nine expresses from London to Nottingham (four with restaurant cars) and eight in the reverse direction (five having facilities for meals). The GCR was faster than the LNWR to Rugby (98 minutes compared with 100 minutes) and it beat the Midland to Leicester (116 minutes as against 120 minutes). When the GCR became part of the London & North Eastern Railway in 1923 it was treated well by receiving Gresley's excellent A3 'Pacifics' for the best trains. These displaced Robinson's beautiful 'Atlantics' and efficient 'Directors' which had been in the habit of exceeding 80 mph on favourable stretches. Robinson had been less happy with his

23

4-6-0 engines, but his 4-6-2Ts were competent on suburban work, which was just as well seeing that Sam Fay had gone to live at Gerrards Cross. The GCR goods engines were very capable—0-6-0 'Pom-Poms', 0-8-0 'Tinies' and the 2-8-0 type. The last were so good that they were chosen by the Government in the 1914 war for standard production. Other types to be seen were Gresley's V2s and Thompson's outstanding B1 4-6-0s (plates 9 and 10). Towards the end of steam there were all kinds—'Royal Scot' 4-6-0s, Stanier Black 5s, BR Standard Class 4 2-6-0s and Class 5 4-6-0s with an occasional 'Britannia' Pacific. When the diesels arrived in 1965 the GCR had to be content with multiple-unit trains of which there were six down and four up between London and Nottingham with four each way between Woodford and Nottingham. Sunday services were limited to one train in each direction.

One accident should be mentioned. On 23rd December 1904 the 2.45 parcels train left Marylebone hauled by a Robinson small 4-4-0 No 1040. The night was foggy and, for some reason never explained, the experienced driver approached the curves leading into Aylesbury station much too fast. The train was derailed, some coaches mounting the platform and others fouling the up road. Immediately after, the 22.20 up Manchester express ran into the wreckage, but fortunately at such a slow speed, due to the fog, that little extra damage was caused. The unfortunate parcels train driver died in hospital. One of the vans of this train had been loaded with Christmas puddings which were spilled all over the track, and it is reported that some of the inhabitants of Aylesbury lent a willing hand in helping to clear these obstructions from the line. Later, Sam Fay persuaded the Metropolitan Railway to ease the curves at that point.

Since the closure, **Nottingham Victoria** station site has been sold for redevelopment, and the section from Rugby to Loughborough has also been disposed of. Nevertheless it is possible to walk along the old track south of **Lutterworth,** although the station itself has disappeared and the track to the north is built over. Try and see the fine church at Lutterworth where John Wycliffe was priest. Catesby Tunnel is perfectly straight and now the smoke has gone one end is visible from the other. The Main Line Steam Trust Ltd has been succeeded by the Great Central Railway (1976) Ltd, and details of their operations will be found in the Appendix. **Charwelton** station, once so busy with iron ore trains, is demolished, as is **Culworth,** but the walking here is good.

The Woodford-Banbury spur is lifted but loose ballast makes the going hard, whereas at **Helmdon** the walking is much better, but you will look in vain for the station. The once pretty **Brackley** station is now occupied as offices but just to the south the great viaduct has been demolished. **Finmere** station is no more, and a little further south the track bed joins the spur put in during the war, and still in use, enabling trains from **Calvert** to run round to Claydon (LNE junction) on the Bletchley-Oxford line. **Quainton Road** must be visited because of the fine collection of locomotives and stock belonging to the Buckinghamshire Railway Centre (see Appendix).

Train: Access to the old lines may be made by train to Aylesbury, Rugby and Leicester.

Buses: Midland Red Nos 633, 643 and 644 serve Leicester, Lutterworth and Rugby. No 754 goes from Lutterworth to Hinckley and No 500 serves Banbury-Brackley-Towcester-Northampton. Nos 494, 506 and 512 are on the Buckingham-Brackley-Banbury route, while the Banbury-Helmdon district can be reached by No 508. The Red Rovers have No 16 Aylesbury-Brackley and No 15 for Aylesbury-Quainton-Calvert.

Car: A5, A6, A43, A361, A413 and A426.

8. YARNTON TO FAIRFORD

Yarnton to Witney: act 1st August 1859; opened 14th November 1861. Witney to Fairford: act 7th August 1862; opened 15th January 1873. Length: 21¾ miles. Closed: 18th June 1962.

That there was considerable support for the construction of the first section of this railway is evident from the prospectus which discloses the promoters to be 'the Magistrates, Clergy and Inhabitants of Witney, the Gentry and Inhabitants of Eynsham and the Corporation of the City of Oxford'. The company was too small to be able to own locomotives and rolling stock so that an arrangement was made with the somewhat threadbare West Midland Railway to work the line. Fortunately for everyone (except the GWR) the West Midland was absorbed by the Great Western on 1st August 1863, although the benefits of this fusion were not immediately apparent. In fact the Witney line's receipts were disappointing and the dividend fell from 2½ per cent to 1 per cent during the first six years and in 1867 a receiver was appointed, his reign lasting eight years. In the meantime the East Gloucester Railway had been opened from Witney to Fairford, but it was not a rich company and was built only as a single line, its bridges being wide enough for one track only. Powers had been obtained to extend the line to Cheltenham where a junction with the Great Western would have proved a great boon, but funds did not permit. When the East Gloucester Railway was opened the GWR worked the whole length from Oxford to Fairford, and the larger company took the branch over as from 1st July 1890.

When first opened the Oxford and Witney line ran four trains each way on weekdays only. This service continued after the extension was opened, the old Witney station being used for goods and a new one sited on the Fairford line a little to the south. Just before the Grouping in 1923, the GWR were running five trains in each direction between Oxford and Fairford, with one on Sundays. Extra stations were opened from time to time to attract custom—Kelmscott in December 1907, Cassington in March 1936 and Carterton in October 1944. The 1939 war brought the usual heavy traffic as Brize Norton airfield was close to the line. The railway ran in very quiet countryside and many of the stations were not well sited; for example, Witney and Fairford were over half a mile from their respective towns. Such a railway was vulnerable during the 1961/2 purge.

For many years the branch was worked by the ubiquitous GWR pannier tanks of the 57xx class, dating from 1929, and their derivatives the 96xx engines (plate 11). There was a turntable at Fairford for tender engines, but tank engines also used it as they filled up with water at the same place.

The line makes pleasant walking not only because of its quiet rural situation but also owing to its historic, literary and architectural associations. It is interesting to record that the famous GWR automatic train control was tried out on the branch in 1906. Today, **Yarnton** station has gone and the site of **Eynsham** is completely built over. Walking is good at **South Leigh** and the attractive weatherboarded station buildings and the brick-built cottage used by former crossing-keepers here are in excellent condition as they are privately occupied. The track is lost at **Witney** where new buildings have obliterated all trace, and it is as well to avoid the noise at **Brize Norton**. The track bed thence is easily found with good going to **Alvescot** where

26

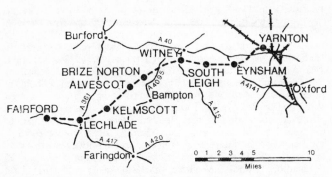

a new bungalow covers the site of the station and the goods yard is now a coal depot. At **Kelmscott & Langford** station the attractively-shaped buildings are demolished but the going is quite good. **Lechlade** station, which once saw the imposing figure of William Morris, consists of platforms only, with easy walking conditions towards Fairford. On the east side of Lechlade the track is now occupied by an electric sub-station. Although **Fairford** station (plate 11) has disappeared under new factory buildings, the walk must be continued to the town where the parish church contains the finest stained glass in England. So splendid is it that special measures were taken for its safety during our own Civil War, and reinstatement took place during the Restoration.

Train: To Oxford.

Bus: South Midland buses—Witney to Abingdon, service No 6; Witney-Bampton-Black Bourton-Alvescot-Langford-Lechlade-Faringdon-Swindon, Nos 468 and 472. Bristol buses—Swindon-Lechlade-Fairford-Cirencester, Nos 472 and 477.

Car: Motorists can reach the district by roads A415 and A417.

9. THE MARQUIS OF EXETER'S RAILWAYS

Stamford to Essendine: act 5th August 1853; opened 1st November 1856; length 4 miles; closed 15th June 1959. Stamford to Wansford: act 25th July 1864; opened 9th August 1867; length 8¼ miles; closed 1st July 1929.

The railway history of Stamford is very similar to that of Northampton in that both succeeded in keeping the new trunk lines at a distance, only to experience a complete change of attitude afterwards. Stamford enjoyed train services at an early date, being connected to Peterborough on 2nd October 1846 and to Melton Mowbray on 1st May 1848. In 1844 the London & York Railway (to become the Great Northern in 1846) had planned to pass through the town but was rebuffed. *The Times* of 29th August 1844 reported: 'The London & York scheme has been totally defeated at a meeting held at Stamford attended by George Stephenson when a vote declared in favour of the Midland and the Eastern Counties Railways'. However, soon after it was deemed necessary to be joined to the GNR main line and the Marquis of Exeter formed a company for the purpose of constructing a railway northwards to Essendine. There was an intermediate station at Ryhall & Belmisthorpe, and the whole line was easily constructed as there were no engineering problems. There was a service in 1867 of nine trains from Stamford (Water Street) to Essendine each weekday and ten in the opposite direction. The 9.50 from Stamford carried third-class passengers on Saturdays only. At Ryhall passengers could be set down if prior notice were given to the guard and those wishing to be taken up had to make clear signals to the driver. There were no Sunday trains. In 1922 there were nine trains each way on weekdays, but still no Sunday trains. Shortly before closure there were four in each direction on weekdays only, but these ran to and from Stamford Town station as Water Street had been closed on 4th March 1957. The GNR worked the line from the start and sent its 0-4-2Ts for the purpose. One of these (No 503) became derailed and fell into the river, after which it was always referred to as 'The Welland Diver'. The GNR leased the branch as from 15th December 1893 and the LNER absorbed it in 1923.

In the early 1860s Stamford was connected with the GNR at Essendine from Water Street, and with Leicester and Peterborough from the Town station. From the latter trains also connected with the Eastern Counties at Peterborough. In 1845 the London & Birmingham Railway had opened a station at Wansford, and after the Essendine line had been opened, the Marquis considered that it would be advantageous to build a branch to Wansford which would provide easy access to Northampton over the LNWR (successors to the LBR). The branch was duly opened with stations at Barnack, Ufford Bridge and Wansford Road, which was the terminus for a short time until junction with the LNWR at Wansford was effected. Ufford Bridge station was not very near Ufford but was conveniently situated for the 'back door' of Burghley

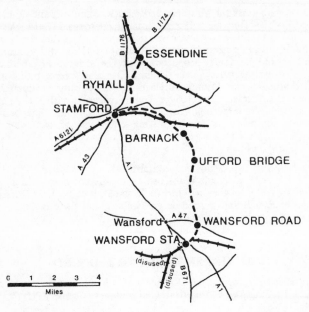

House. After leaving Water Street the railway climbed so as to be able to cross the Midland by an overline bridge near Barnack. It then ran south finally curving west to form a junction at Wansford. Like its Essendine partner it was single throughout but with enough land for future doubling and the usual passing places. The GNR worked the line for twenty-one years and then leased it until 1923 when the LNER took it over. At the outset six trains ran from Stamford to Wansford and five in the return direction on weekdays only, Sunday being a day of rest. In 1929 the number had decreased to four each way, weekdays only, and the line's early decease indicates that the Exeter family had little use for it. The decision to close was made by the LNER, possibly because the only useful station was Barnack, the remainder being remote. Both lines in later years were worked by Ivatt's pretty C12 4-4-2Ts of the former GNR (plate 13).

The track beds in each case are suitable for walking and on a fine day provide excellent exploration. If there is time, on no account miss the churches at Barnack, Stamford and Wansford, while Burghley House (open Tuesdays, Wednesdays, Thursdays and Saturdays) must be seen. The buildings at **Stamford East** station (formerly Water Street) are still standing and should be visited on account of the striking Elizabethan style of architecture (plates 12 and 13). The station buildings at Stamford and **Wansford Road** are in private occupation. Near the former, the George Inn is worth a visit, while at Wansford the Haycock Inn is deservedly famous. The Nene Valley Railway has an interesting collection of locomotives and stock, which are referred to in the Appendix.

Train: To Stamford.

Bus: Barton No 3 bus from Stamford to Wansford. The 17 and 17a services reach Wansford by a different route. On Fridays bus No 1a goes to Ufford. Delaine buses go from Stamford to Ryhall and Essendine on Fridays, and there is a service from Stamford to Bourne.

Car: Motorists can take the A1, the A47 and the A43 roads.

10. HORSHAM TO GUILDFORD

Act: 1864. Opened: 2nd October 1865. Length (Christ's Hospital to Peasmarsh Junction): 15¾ miles. Closed: 12th June 1965.

The enterprise of railway promoters in the nineteenth century resulted in the vast network of lines, which as recently as 1950 was still intact. In the south of the country the Horsham & Guildford Direct Railway Company was formed in 1860 but found difficulty in raising the required capital. The result was that it was taken over by the London, Brighton & South Coast Railway which, having obtained an act in 1864, opened the line a year later. The branch therefore broke the monopoly which the London & South Western Railway had hitherto enjoyed in connection with Guildford, although as it was laid to branch line standards, it included some steep gradients. From the old Stammerham Junction, now Christ's Hospital, the line climbed at 1 in 60 at Slinfold after which there was a slight easing to 1 in 80. The bridges over the river Arun at Rudgwick and the Wey near Peasmarsh Junction were not strong enough to carry a locomotive heavier than a Q1 0-6-0, and because the tunnel at Baynards (381 yards) was a wet one, some trains tended to stall in it. The line ran through pretty country, and the stations, with the possible exception of Slinfold, were near the places they served. Mention must be

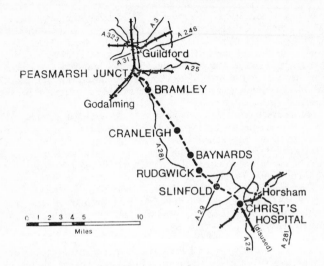

made of Baynards station which was built to cater for Baynards Park, the home of Lord Thurlow. During the latter years of the line's existence the station was a blaze of colour during the summer months thanks to the efforts of the signalman who was an expert gardener and his display of dahlias was, as Dr Johnson would have said, 'not only worth seeing but worth going to see'.

In 1865 the LB&SCR ran three trains on weekdays and two on Sundays. The service was gradually improved until in 1922 (the last year before Grouping) it consisted of six down trains and seven up, with three each way on Sundays. In 1965 six trains ran in each direction on weekdays only. This delightful branch suffered from the fact that it ran through a quiet and sparsely populated countryside. The station at Christ's Hospital did not bring in the income which had been expected not only from the possible spread of the town of Horsham but also from the nearby Edward VI school, Christ's Hospital, which had moved from London in 1902. The station was opened on 28th April that year, but was busy only when the school's terms commenced and ended.

The first engine on the branch was a 2-2-2 No 30 which worked until 1886; next came the Stroudley D1 0-4-2Ts and the Billinton D3 0-4-4Ts. Later years saw the Drummond

M7 0-4-4Ts and the Wainwright H class of the same wheel arrangement. Goods traffic was handled by 0-6-0s of the C2x, Q and Q1 classes. The excellent Ivatt 2-6-2Ts (plate 14) took over during the last decade and it was No 41287 of this class which hauled the last train almost a hundred years after the opening of the line. This was one of those branches which could not stand up to the Beeching type of scrutiny, however useful it may have been.

This quiet line has not been entirely without excitement. In 1940, when an enemy aircraft attempted to rake a train with machine-gun fire, the driver was able to reach the safety of Baynards Tunnel without serious damage to engine and coaches. More recently the television film version of *The Railway Children* was made on this branch with the help of a Drummond T9 4-4-0 No 30126. There is only one recorded accident—not serious—which occurred at Bramley & Wonersh station when a train ran into the buffer stops through a signalman's error.

The walker will find that there is much to interest him. The track is accessible from **Christ's Hospital** station but it is more rewarding to take the train to Guildford whence there are plenty of buses. A good plan is to take a bus to Wonersh where you can walk either to Peasmarsh Junction or in the other direction to Cranleigh (plate 14). **Bramley** station buildings have recently been demolished. The track bed is good but the bridges have gone. Pony riders are beginning to use the track and anglers find it provides short cuts to rivers and ponds. Finally, try and see the parish churches at Guildford and Horsham, and if you like modern architecture Guildford cathedral has much to offer.

Train: To Guildford or Christ's Hospital.

Bus: From Guildford Alder Valley services Nos 33 to Bramley, Cranleigh and Horsham, 49 to Bramley and Wisborough Green, 23 to Bramley, Shamley Green, Cranleigh and Ewhurst, 25 to Cranleigh via Smithwood Common.

Car: Motorists should choose the road A281.

11. LEWES & EAST GRINSTEAD RAILWAY

Acts: 1877 and 1878. Opened: 1st August 1882. Closed: 28th May 1955. Reopened: 7th August 1956. Closed: 16th March 1958. Length: 20¼ miles.

1. Halwill Junction: Maunsell N class 2-6-0 31839 on the 16.05 to Okehampton, 9th May 1958.

2. Launceston: the former L&SWR station with a WR train leaving for Plymouth. The old GWR station is on the left of the picture.

3. *Tipton St John: Drummond M7 0-4-4T 30024 on the 13.56 Sidmouth Junction to Exmouth, 11th May 1961.*

4. *South Molton: GWR 43xx 2-6-0 7337 hauling a Barnstaple train, waiting to cross a Taunton train, 8th May 1961.*

5. Highbridge: LMR class 3 0-6-0 43248 (S&DR 75) at the head of the 14.20 to Templecombe, 3rd May 1958.

6. Blandford Forum: BR standard class 9 2-10-0 92220 'Evening Star' bringing in the 15.40 Bournemouth West to Bath on 17th August 1963. This engine was the last steam locomotive to be built at Swindon.

7. Old North Road: LNER J17 (GER F48) 0-6-0 65556 shunting, March 1960. This station always had a colourful display of flowers.

8. Old North Road, 1973. The buildings and land were sold for private occupation for £25,000.

9. Woodford Halse: Thompson B1 4-6-0 61206 on the 13.15 Nottingham to Marylebone train, 31st August 1961. Note the changing of the engine crew.

10. Brackley: right away for Nottingham. B1 61106 about to leave on the 13.37, 24th July 1961.

11. Fairford: GWR 0-6-0PT just arrived with the 12.15 from Oxford, 18th May 1961. Note the wedge-shaped signal box.

12. Stamford (Water Street): the imposing station building designed for the Marquis of Exeter's railway.

13. Stamford (Water Street) on last day of working, 2nd March 1957. Ivatt C12 4-4-2T 67376 on the 13.05 to Essendine, with Jack Day at the regulator.

14. Cranleigh: a sturdy Ivatt LMS class 2 2-6-2T 41326 at the head of the 17.04 train from Guildford crosses 41325 on the 16.53 from Horsham, 29th September 1963.

15. Sheffield Park: E4 0-6-2T 473 'Birch Grove', designed by R. J. Billinton, arriving at Sheffield Park in July 1970. This engine has been restored by the Bluebell Railway Preservation Society.

16. Class G5 0-4-4T 67345 near Crake Hall on the Northallerton to Garsdale line in 1954. W. Worsdell's design dates from 1894 and was Class O in NER days. This engine was originally numbered 435.

J. W. Armstrong

17. *White Colne: a two-car d.m.u., the 13.57 from Haverhill, departing for Mark's Tey, 28th April 1961. Note the old carriage body used as a waiting room.*

18. *Yeldham, Colne Valley Railway. The disused grain store has now been dismantled and erected on a new site by the CVR.*

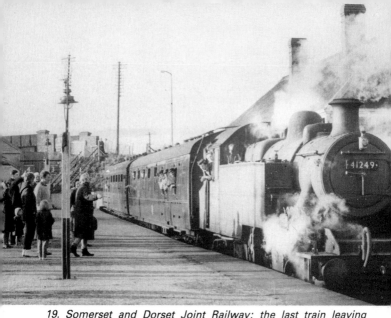

19. *Somerset and Dorset Joint Railway: the last train leaving Highbridge at 16.00 for Evercreech Junction on 5 March 1966. The engine is Ivatt Class 2 2-6-2T No. 41249.*

20. *North Norfolk Railway: GER Class Y14 0-6-0 (LNER J15) 564 at the pretty Weybourne station on its recommissioning day.*

Brian Fisher

21. *The Churnet Valley line of the NSR was famous for its beautiful stations. This is the attractive stone edifice at Cheddleton, looking towards Leek, 1973. The single line is for mineral traffic.*

22. *Alton Towers: Pugin's little gem on the Churnet Valley Railway, 1973.*

23. *Cardington: the 13.52 for Hitchin leaves behind Stanier class 3 2-6-2T 40165 on 26th June 1957, the line's centenary year.*

24. *Norbury & Ellaston: looking towards Buxton, 1973. The station is now converted into a most attractive dwelling.*

25. Praised by Sir John Betjeman, an exquisite station lamp at Wolferton, 1973.
C. W. Collard

26. Wolferton: the beautifully preserved signal-box is complete with levers and frame and the railway cottages are in excellent preservation (1973).

C. W. Collard

27. The graceful viaduct at Cwm Prysor, halfway between Blaenau Ffestiniog and Bala, September 1953.

J. J. Davis

28. Bedale: view from the goods yard showing excellent NER station buildings, beautifully maintained and with beds of flowers, 1973.

29. Leyburn: with the passing loop in good order it is difficult to realise that passenger trains ceased in 1954. View looking towards Hawes, 1973.

30. Class D20 4-4-0 62347 at Hawes in 1950. Originally NER class R no. 1672, built by W. Worsdell in 1907, this locomotive was shedded at Northallerton in BR days.
J. W. Armstrong

31. Bala Lake Railway: Hunslet 0-4-0ST 'Maid Marian' at Llanuwchllyn station with two new corridor bogie coaches. Note the GWR signal-box. The station buildings are the only Bala-Dolgellau structures in existence.
P. Briddon

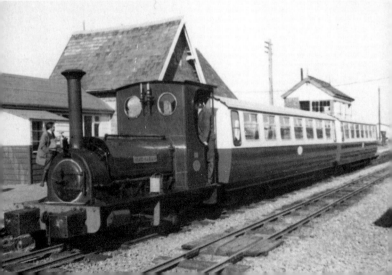

This line, formerly a branch of the London Brighton & South Coast Railway and referred to as the 'Bluebell Line', had the rare distinction of being opened and closed twice. Promoted by the Earl of Sheffield and Lord de la Warr, the original scheme envisaged a line from Lewes to London via East Grinstead, but the financial burden proved too great and the help of the LB&SCR had to be invoked. As a result, a shorter line was built from Lewes to East Grinstead with double track between Horsted Keynes and East Grinstead, and provision for double track between Horsted Keynes and Lewes, although this portion remained single. The geography of Sussex and the need to keep the expense of construction within reasonable bounds resulted in many gradients of 1 in 75 and engineering works included the Imberhorne viaduct just south of East Grinstead, the Sharpthorne tunnel south of West Hoathly and another tunnel near Newick station called Cinder Hill.

On the opening of the railway five trains were run in each direction on weekdays with two Sunday trains. In 1887 the number of weekday trains was increased to seven. The line throve in a modest way for the first forty years, enjoying a heavy trade from farm produce, particularly milk, and a reasonable passenger traffic, augmented in season by the famous cricket matches at Sheffield Park and Volunteers' field days. In the last days of the LB&SCR as an individual company (1922) the passenger service consisted of six down and seven up trains, Sundays still having two. After the 1939 war there was a decline in traffic but as the BTC made a profit until 1954 it was not until the following year that the decision was made. This occurred on 28th May, but a local resident, Miss Bessemer, was aware that the original Act included a clause requiring four passenger trains to be run daily in perpetuity. She was therefore successful in having the service restored although Kingscote and Barcombe stations remained closed as they were not mentioned in the Act. The revived service lasted only eighteen months. In 1959 the Bluebell Railway Preservation Society was formed and presently it operates a service between Sheffield Park and Horsted Keynes, carrying over 300,000 passengers a year. The remainder of the track was lifted in August 1964.

Since this book was first published certain changes have taken place in the occupation of land to the north of Horsted Keynes station. The land is now occupied privately and walkers can no longer use the old track bed. Nevertheless a pleasant day can be spent by first visiting Sheffield Park gardens, owned

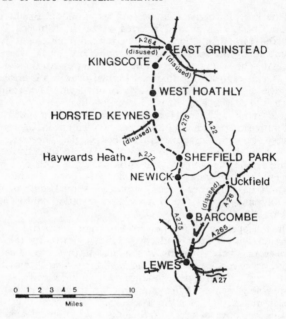

by the National Trust, followed by a trip on the Bluebell Railway from Sheffield Park to Horsted Keynes and back.

At Sheffield Park station (plate 15) the Bluebell Railway has an excellent collection of steam locomotives, all of which are kept in first-class repair in the workshops. The truly LB&SCR atmosphere is preserved by two Terrier tank engines, *Stepney* and *Fenchurch*, the latter dating from 1872. It is therefore the oldest standard-gauge steam engine in service which was formerly owned by one of the leading companies. A third LB&SC locomotive is *Birch Grove*, an E4 0-6-2T engine. Other tank engines are three P class of Wainwright's SE&CR design, a North London 0-6-0T No 2650, the famous Adams radial tank No 488 from the former L&SWR, and a US Army 'switcher' or 0-6-0T. There are some powerful tender engines such as former GWR 4-4-0 *Earl of Berkeley*, BR standard Class 4 No 75027, and the useful SE&CR C class No 592. The Bulleid Society has brought its West Country Pacific, *Blackmore Vale*, into service. Lastly there are five small industrial tank engines. (See Appendix.)

In 1986 planning permission was granted to the railway for an extension from Horsted Keynes to East Grinstead.

Train: To Lewes or East Grinstead.

Bus: To visit the southern part of the line one can take the No 19 bus from Lewes to Newick or the 20 to Chailey. The 87 bus from East Grinstead and the 30 bus from Brighton serve Horsted Keynes village, whence a pleasant walk of 1½ miles brings one to the station. These services are provided by the Southdown Company.

Car: Motorists should follow the A275 to Sheffield Park station.

12. TUNBRIDGE WELLS & EASTBOURNE RAILWAY

Polegate to Hailsham: act 18th June 1846, opened 14th May 1849, closed 8th September 1968. Eridge to Hailsham: act 5th August 1873, opened 1st September 1880, closed 14th June 1965. Length (Eridge to Polegate): 20½ miles.

One of the last moves of the London & Brighton Railway (which became the LB&SCR on 27th July 1846) was to obtain an Act to permit the construction of a line from Eastbourne to Hailsham, and trains began to run on this short section in 1849. Thirty years later a scheme was proposed to join Hailsham to Eridge where there had been a station since 1868 and thus provide a direct route between Eastbourne and Tunbridge Wells. Before the opening date the venture had been absorbed by the LB&SCR (1876) to enlarge their empire and to protect themselves against the perennial threat of the South Eastern Railway. The branch in due course became known as the 'Cuckoo Line' after the Cuckoo Fair held annually at Heathfield on 14th April. Hailsham might have been an important junction had the LB&SCR built their Ouse Valley line from the viaduct north of Haywards Heath across to Uckfield, Hailsham and St Leonards. The powers obtained in 1864 were hampered by the national financial crisis of 1866 and two years later the project was abandoned.

The Cuckoo Line was single throughout with overline bridges wide enough for two tracks. Gradients were fairly severe as, for example, the fall at 1 in 88 from Redgate Mill junction towards Rotherfield. There were two short tunnels, the longer, just north of Heathfield being 200 yards. In the years after the opening throughout there were seven trains each way on weekdays, with one additional train between Heathfield and

Eastbourne, and two on Sundays. This service continued through the years and the number of trains was unchanged at the Grouping. Despite the difficulties after 1945 the service was maintained and even improved, as British Rail were running thirteen trains in each direction in 1964, with seven on Sundays. The railway had been viewed with disfavour by Dr Beeching, and although Mayfield and Hailsham stations were conveniently placed, it must be admitted that the remainder were somewhat remote from the villages they were intended to serve. In 1880 this was not such a defect, as the public would regard it as normal to take a horse-drawn conveyance to and from the station.

The first engines on the branch were Craven 2-4-0Ts which were duly replaced by Stroudley D1 0-4-2Ts and one particular E1 0-6-0T named *Barcelona*, No 157. From 1892 the D3 0-4-4-Ts designed by R. J. Billinton appeared, and after 1923 Wainwright's H class 0-4-4Ts were to be seen on the Cuckoo Line as indeed they were all over the south-east of the Southern Railway system. After 1951 the excellent BR standard 2-6-4Ts, built at Brighton, took over. In due course, diesel multiple-unit trains supplemented steam, but for the last runs on 12th June 1965 BR sportingly produced No 80144 to do the honours.

On 1st September 1897 a derailment occurred between Heathfield and Mayfield. The 8.18 from Eastbourne was being hauled by D1 0-4-2T No 297 *Bonchurch* when it left the track, followed by the six coaches. The driver was unfortunately killed, but there were no other casualties. It was considered that the track was not substantial enough for high-speed running.

Although the southern part of the line is easy of access, the explorer should choose the northern half as it is much prettier. The road A26 passes **Eridge** station and footpaths from it lead to Redgate Mill Junction (railway milepost 25¾). The old track bed is ballasted at first but the surface soon improves and there follows a delightful walk to **Rotherfield**. Here the station buildings are occupied and the land is private, but the course of the railway can be resumed thereafter through pretty wooded countryside to **Mayfield**. The gaps left in the track by the demolished bridges do not present any real obstacle and the walk is recommended for that rare thing today—complete quiet. If time permits the church at Heathfield and the Middle House inn at Mayfield are well worth a visit.

Train: To visit the line the railway enthusiast will naturally go by train, and he has the choice of Eridge whence the track

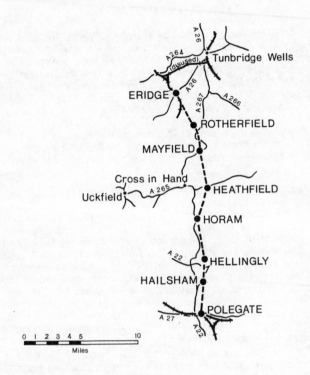

bed can be attained by footpaths, or Polegate with direct access.

Bus: The Southdown Company caters very well thus: Eastbourne to Polegate, services 15, 94, 190 and 191. The last two services also go to Horam and Heathfield. Uckfield can be reached by Nos 92, 190 and 191, and here the Maidstone & District buses 119 and 219 go to Eridge station. This company provides a service from Tunbridge Wells, No 152 going to Heathfield.

Car: A car, of course, gives the greatest flexibility and road A267 follows the course of the railway closely.

13. STRATFORD-ON-AVON & MIDLAND JUNCTION RAILWAY

East & West Junction Railway (Green's Norton Junction to Stratford-on-Avon): act 23rd June 1864; opened, Fenny Compton to Kineton 1st June 1871, Kineton to Stratford-on-Avon 1st July 1873, Fenny Compton to Green's Norton 1st July 1873. Evesham Redditch & Stratford-on-Avon Junction Railway: act 5th August 1873; opened 2nd June 1879. Easton Neston Mineral & Towcester Roade & Olney Junction Railway: act 15th August 1879; opened 13th April 1891. Closed: Stratford to Broom 16th June 1947, Blisworth to Banbury 2nd July 1951, Stratford to Blisworth 5th April 1952, Ravenstone Junction to Towcester (goods) 22nd June 1958, Stratford to Broom (goods) June 1960.

The faith of the Victorians in their railway system and their determination to overcome almost insuperable difficulties are exemplified in the history of the E&WJR. That the line was not lacking in influential support will be gathered from the presence of Lady Palmerston at the ceremony of cutting the first sod on 3rd August 1864. But the company had difficulty in raising capital from the general public, a fact which can be understood when it is realised that, even today, the countryside is sparsely inhabited. However it was not passenger traffic which interested the railway so much as the conveyance of iron ore from Northamptonshire to South Wales; this was dense enough in time of war but suffered from continental competition in peaceful years.

Both passenger and goods traffic on the E&WJR failed to come up to expectations and the company's financial position became so weak that a receiver was appointed on 29th January 1875, and he decided to withdraw passenger services as from 31st July 1877. Eight years elapsed before the line next saw a passenger train. The E&WJR had secured running powers over the Northampton & Banbury Railway (opened Blisworth to Banbury on 1st June 1872), so that its trains could reach Blisworth station, but these powers did not fend off disaster. In the meantime services were running on the Evesham Redditch & Stratford Railway so that when passenger trains again appeared on the E&WJR it was possible to organise services between Blisworth E&WJ and Broom Junction ER&SJ. This arrangement began on 22nd March 1885.

At the other end of the system, the Easton Neston company had changed its name to the Stratford Towcester & Midland

Junction (1887) but it had to wait another four years before its first trains ran over the Midland, from Ravenstone Wood Junction to Olney. These were goods only, but an attempt to give a passenger service lasted only four months—1st December 1892 to 1st April 1893. It is not possible in the space available, to record every small development on these railways, but it can be mentioned that fresh acts were obtained from time to time for the purpose of raising more capital. The larger companies, that is to say, the L&NWR, the GWR and the Midland, had blown hot and cold in their dealings with their small neighbours, but in 1899 the enterprising Great Central gave much needed help by means of a spur from Woodford GCR to Byfield ST&MJ. The twentieth century witnessed a great improvement. By an act dated 1st August 1908 more capital was obtained, the name was altered to Stratford-on-Avon & Midland Junction Railway to cover the three small entities and running powers were granted to the four large neighbours—GCR, MR, GWR, and L&NWR. On 29th April 1910 the old Northampton & Banbury Railway was taken over with a resulting total route mileage of seventy, and the railway was now advertised as the 'Shakespeare Route'. The following year the management was enterprising enough to instal the 'Railophone' on one of their trains whereby passengers could speak by telephone from a moving train. On 1st January 1923 the SMJ became part of the LMS and three years later the freight traffic was augmented by the running of the well-known 'banana specials' from Avonmouth docks to St Pancras via Broom and Ravenstone Wood junctions. 1931 saw the opening of the Welcombe Hotel at Stratford, served partly by the new 'Roadrailer' which ran on the railway from Blisworth to Stratford and, by an ingenious mechanism, pursued its course by road to the hotel running on rubber-tyred wheels. To serve this hotel a fast train was run from Stratford to Blisworth in 62 minutes, a creditable performance over 38¼ miles of single line. Passenger traffic was increased when there was a race meeting at Towcester by the running of special trains from St Pancras. The 1939 war brought so much military traffic that a south curve was put in at Broom Junction to save the reversal of trains from Avonmouth, this dating from 28th September 1942. After 1950 there was the usual story of declining traffic and the SMJ was hardly the line to stand up to the climate of opinion which has prevailed since.

Engineering works consisted of a three-span girder bridge over the river Arrow near Bidford and a very deep cutting just west of Kineton. From Towcester to Blisworth the line

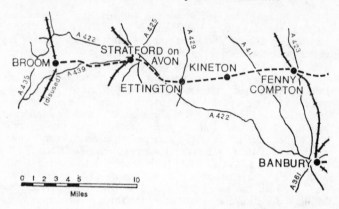

climbed at 1 in 75 and there was an ascent for west-bound trains at 1 in 101 near Byfield. At Kineton these trains would descend at 1 in 98. On the Banbury line the worst gradient was from Wappenham up to Helmdon summit at 1 in 65.

In 1876 there were two trains each way between Blisworth and Stratford; in 1920 one in each direction between Blisworth and Broom and two between Stratford and Blisworth. By 1947 the services had been increased between Stratford and Broom to four each way daily, and on the Stratford to Blisworth section three each way. The Towcester to Banbury branch had only two trains in each direction on weekdays only. The SMJ never ran Sunday trains and, like so many railways, relied on its goods traffic.

The railway owned a total of thirty-one locomotives of such various origins that it is impossible to give details. The line can be easily explored from Ravenstone Wood Junction. **Salcey Forest** station, used during the 1939 war to house evacuees from London, has now been demolished, but **Stoke Bruerne** station buildings are intact and privately occupied. Nearby is the British Waterways museum. The section from Towcester to Banbury is good for walking, although **Wappenham** station has gone and **Helmdon** site is built over. Westwards to Stratford upon Avon is suitable for exploration, but the stations have mostly gone. At **Moreton Pinkney** and **Byfield** the platforms and outbuildings are all that is left.

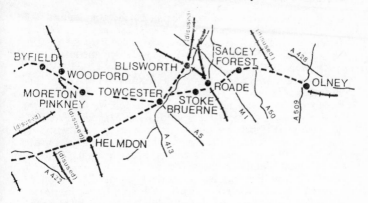

Train: Stratford-on-Avon station can be reached by rail, otherwise the visit must be made by road.

Bus: Midland Red service Nos 500 for Banbury, Brackley, Towcester, and Northampton; 494 and 506 for Buckingham, Brackley and Banbury; 512 Banbury to Brackley; 508 Brackley to Helmdon; 524 and 538 Evesham to Stratford; 518 and 590 for Warwick, Leamington and Stratford; 530 for Ettington; 530 and 531 for Kineton; 533 Leamington to Fenny Compton. United Counties No 346 for Northampton, Towcester and Buckingham.

Car: Take the A5 road for Towcester and the A34 for Stratford.

14. WARE HADHAM & BUNTINGFORD RAILWAY

Act: 12th July 1858.   Opened: 3rd July 1863.   Length: 13¾ miles. Closed: 16th November 1964.

Very soon after construction had begun, George Mickley and Richard Wren of Buntingford, and C. H. Ellis of Wyddial Hall, the promoters of the railway, found that money had run out. Although there was plenty of enthusiasm the necessary capital was hard to come by, but the Eastern Counties Railway promised to assist. However, this company had plenty of work on hand as it was about to unite with the East Anglian, Newmarket, Eastern Union and Norfolk Railways to form the Great Eastern Railway. As soon as royal assent was obtained on 7th August 1862, the completion of the Buntingford line was placed on the agenda of the GER, but as its motto was *festina lente* for the first few years, it was not until 1st September 1868 that the GER purchased the little line, the total outlay being £75,000.

There are no great engineering features on the line. The river Lea is crossed by a girder bridge soon after St Margarets, but as economy was necessary the route follows the lie of the land with such gradients as 1 in 56 near Standon. From the commencement there were four trains each way on weekdays with two on Sundays, passengers being enjoined as regards Mardock, Widford and Westmill stations to warn the guard or to signal plainly to the driver for the purposes of setting down and picking up respectively. Towards the end of its existence the GER had increased the weekly service to ten trains up and down, Sunday still having two. Under British Rail just before closure there were nine trains each way, and no Sunday service.

For many years the trains had the typical GER branch-line appearance, that is old six-wheel stock hauled by Holden's M15 2-4-2Ts. Two of these were stationed at Buntingford shed, No 578 being there for many years. Later the L&NER version of Hill's efficient 0-6-2Ts (GER L77 class) dealt with the traffic, and from 15th June 1959 the diesel multiple-unit trains took over. The line was marked down for closure during the fateful 1961/2 period and duly succumbed in the purge for economy although lying within the 'commuter belt'. It filled the gap between the GNR Cambridge branch and the GER main line but would have benefited from an extension to Royston, on the former.

If the traveller takes the electric train from Liverpool Street to St Margarets he will soon pick up the trail and will find it very pleasant going over the Lea and on to Water Place. This is shown as a public footpath. Some of the villages en route have all the quiet beauty for which much of the Hertfordshire countryside is celebrated. **Widford** is an example. The station, now gone, was nearly a mile from the village and there is excellent walking to be had for some distance on each side. At this point the line is going in a north-easterly direction. Incidentally Widford is the town 'W' mentioned in Lamb's *Essays*. Near **Hadham** the track has been obliterated and wheat now grows where trains once ran. Truly *seges est ubi Troja fuit*. Much Hadham village is well worth going to see but Hadham station is a ruin and it is best to push on to **Standon** although the station here has been demolished. Exploration

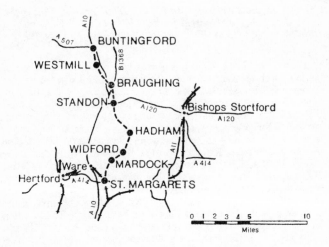

is still feasible at **Braughing** but near **Westmill** the track bed is buried beneath the widened road A10. There is no trace of the station. At **Buntingford** the station buildings are occupied as offices but still have the GER touch. Sir Albert Richardson, a former PRA, praised the architecture of the inns at Buntingford, Much Hadham, Stanstead Abbots (which is near St Margarets) and Ware. They are all worth a visit if time permits.

Train: To St Margarets.

Bus: Green Line coach No 724 runs from Harlow to Hertford via St Margarets. London Country buses 350 and 350a run from Hertford to Bishops Stortford via Hadham and Widford. No 331 serves the Buntingford to Hertford route, and No 386 goes from Hitchin to Hertford via Standon. Buses 331 and 331a go from Ware to Buntingford.

Car: Motorists will find the A10, A120 and A507 roads suitable.

15. COLNE VALLEY & HALSTEAD RAILWAY

Chappel to Halstead: act 30th June 1856, opened 16th April 1860. Halstead to Haverhill: act 13th August 1859, opened 10th May 1863. Length: 19 miles. Closed: 1st January 1962.

It was the Stour Valley Railway which built the beautiful viaduct over the river Colne near Chappel, and a train service commenced between Mark's Tey and Sudbury on 11th July 1849. The act empowered the company to build a line to Halstead but this part of the scheme was dropped. This town, having a thriving silk-weaving industry, obviously required a railway, but it had to wait another eleven years. The Colne Valley & Halstead Railway formed a junction with the Stour Valley line at Chappel turning away west to Earl's Colne, Halstead and Haverhill, where for many years it had a station separate from that of the Great Eastern. The GER arrived in Haverhill in August 1865 by a route of twenty-five miles compared with the Colne Valley's nineteen miles. Trains often left Chappel within a few minutes of each other but the CV&H train arrived in Haverhill a good ten minutes before the rival GER. Actually the competition was not damaging as the CV&HR throve by being able to derive traffic from Cambridge and Colchester over the lines of the GER. The little railway was never rich, however, and had to build its line fairly cheaply with resulting gradients of 1 in 70/80 from Haverhill down to Birdbrook, with a climb at the other end from Chappel to White Colne at 1 in 60.

It is notable that this railway maintained its independence until the Grouping of 1st January 1923. At that time it had five locomotives, thirteen passenger and 174 goods vehicles. One engine dated from 1877 being a 0-4-2T from Neilsons. There were also engines of the 2-4-2T type by Hawthorn Leslie of 1887 manufacture and a more modern Hudswell Clark 0-6-2T made in 1908. Passenger rolling stock consisted mostly of discarded GER six-wheel coaches and also three-bogie vehicles which had done good service on the Metropolitan District railway. The minor stations were simply built like Birdbrook and White Colne which were of timber, and Yeldham —part brick and part timber. White Colne had, as a waiting room, a fascinating old carriage body dating from the early days of the line (plate 17). It was worth alighting at the station just to inspect this ancient relic with its untouched interior, seats and all. Halstead had a fine brick-built station.

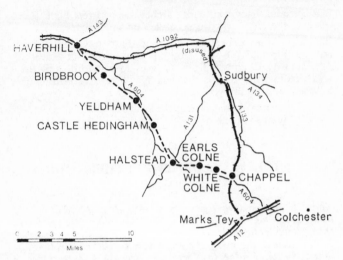

From the start there were three trains on weekdays from Chappel to Haverhill and four in the opposite direction. Sunday trains numbered two each way and this service was maintained up to the end of the railway's independent existence. In 1961 the number of trains to Haverhill had been increased to five, still with four to Chappel and two on Sundays. The closure was of course a great blow to regular travellers and those without cars suffered most. The replacement buses are indicated below.

Walking the track from **Haverhill** is reasonably good, being in the open country, and more weedy in the station areas. Although the station buildings have mostly been demolished, and the underline bridges are down, the going is quite good and between **Yeldham** (plate 18) and **Hedingham** the track bed has been designated a public footpath by one local authority.

Go and see the fine late-Norman church at **Castle Hedingham**. At Chappel station yard the East Anglian Railway Museum has a collection of locomotives and rolling stock, while at Castle Hedingham the Colne Valley Railway Co Ltd has moved and rebuilt Castle Hedingham station.

Train: The best way to see the line is to travel by train from Liverpool Street to Chappel as the train will take you over that splendid viaduct of thirty arches, each 75 feet high. From Chappel the old track can be picked up immediately.

Bus: From the Cambridge direction Eastern Counties buses Nos 59, 113 and 136 will drop one conveniently at Haverhill. At Sudbury, Chambers's bus 6x goes to Haverhill and there is a Hedingham & District bus No 4 serving Hedingham, Yeldham and Sudbury.

Car: The visitor should choose the road A604 which runs near the railway most of the time.

16. MIDLAND & GREAT NORTHERN JOINT RAILWAY

Norwich & Spalding Railway: act 4th August 1853; opened from Holbeach to Spalding 15th November 1858; closed throughout 28th February 1959. Length: Little Bytham to Sutton Bridge 30 miles, Peterborough to Sutton Bridge, 27½ miles, Sutton Bridge to Yarmouth Beach 82¼ miles, Melton Constable to Norwich City 21¼ miles, Melton Constable to Cromer Beach 15 miles. Total 176 miles.

This great cross-country railway, stretching from the Midlands to the Norfolk coast, took forty-eight years to complete because it was built in small sections at a time. Between 1858 and 1906 no fewer than nineteen small lengths were built by various companies—Norwich & Spalding, Lynn & Sutton, Spalding & Bourne, Peterborough Wisbech & Sutton, Great Yarmouth & Stalham, Lynn & Fakenham and the Yarmouth & North Norfolk Railways. On 18th August 1882 some of these united to form the Eastern & Midland Railway which extended its line from Melton to North Walsham on 5th April 1883. Further expansion was from Melton to Holt on 1st October 1884, Cromer being reached on 16th June 1887. Other amalgamations resulted in the Midland & Great Northern Railway Act of 9th June 1893 when the Spalding avoiding line was opened, and Bourne was connected to Little Bytham on 1st May 1894. On the same day, the Midland completed the line Saxby-Little Bytham. After forty years of warfare the M&GN came to terms with the Great Eastern, and the result was the formation of the Norfolk & Suffolk Joint Railways Committee which was able to promote branches which neither company, separately, would have deemed justifiable. For example, on 1st July 1898 the North Walsham to Mundesley line was opened. Further extensions were Yarmouth to Lowestoft over the imposing bridge crossing Breydon Water (13th July 1903) and the Mundesley branch was extended to Cromer Beach on 3rd August 1906. This is a very brief summary of the company's history.

This part of England does not present any great engineering problems and there was only one tunnel, which was 1½ miles west of Bourne and had a length of 330 yards. The crossing of the principal rivers involved the construction of substantial bridges—a swing bridge over the Nene at Sutton Bridge, and the long Clenchwarton bridge over the Great Ouse near South Lynn. This bridge was in need of costly repairs in 1959 and it is thought that this expense was a factor in the decision to close the line. The large expanse of Breydon Water required a steel viaduct and a swing bridge. There were some trying gradients: 1 in 56 for 14 chains up to North Walsham going east; 1 in 100 at three places—Bourne up to Little Bytham, this for two miles; Grimston up to Massingham for the same distance, and Fakenham up to Thursford for four miles. The railway was single for 109 miles of the total.

In 1893 the new M&GN ran five trains from South Lynn to Yarmouth Beach and four in the reverse direction each weekday. On Sundays there was one train in each direction. Fast trains took 2 hours 32 minutes for the trip while an all-stations train required 3 hours 24 minutes. By 1914 two trains had been put on each weekday from Birmingham to Yarmouth. In 1920 the Sunday trains had been withdrawn but weekdays saw six each way between Lynn and Yarmouth. There was then a train which left South Lynn at 13.08 calling only at Melton, Aylsham and North Walsham, arriving at Yarmouth at 15.15, and in the westwards direction the 13.22 from Yarmouth reached South Lynn at 15.41. Improvements were gradually made in the services so that by 1936 a train left Manchester at 10.50 and arrived at Cromer at 17.22. This was Saturdays only and included a restaurant car. Just before the closure there were only four trains each way between Lynn and Yarmouth, and none on Sundays.

Much has been written about the locomotives of this interesting railway. The early Lynn & Fakenham engines were painted green, but after the Joint Railway was formed the livery adopted for passenger engines was 'golden ochre' (darker than the Brighton yellow), with a dark chocolate for goods. The first locomotives were 2-2-2s supplied by either the Midland or the GNR, but the line was better known for the Beyer

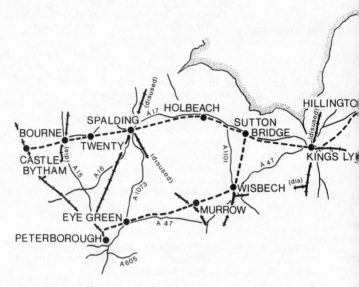

Peacock 4-4-0s with outside cylinders and the Johnson 4-4-0s with inside cylinders. As from 1897 the works at Melton Constable built a number of tank engines, mostly 0-6-0 and some very handsome 4-4-2Ts as well. Between the wars visitors to the Broads cannot fail to have seen the 4-4-0s going over the bridge at Potter Heigham. In 1905 an 0-6-0T with outside cylinders was produced by Melton, later numbered 16, being one of the last to survive, still shunting at South Lynn in 1947. Subsequently LNER 4-4-0s (D16) and 4-6-0s (B12) were seen, but in the later years the train haulage was monopolised by Ivatt's excellent 2-6-0s. At South Lynn shed (31D) there were Nos 43093/4, 43108, 43110, 43148 and 43150/1. Yarmouth Beach (32F) had 43157/8 and 43161. With four coaches these handy engines had no difficulty in keeping time, working up to 56 mph between the frequent stops.

The line was full of interest. Aylsham was notable for its colourful flower-beds on the platforms; Melton Constable had a good refreshment room and formerly a private waiting room for Lord Hastings. There were unusual station names like Twenty and Counter Drain between Spalding and Bourne.

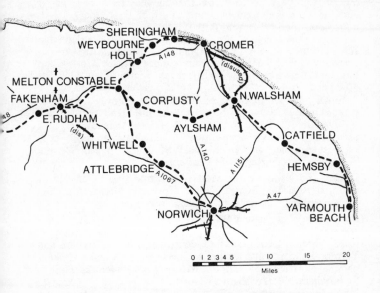

At the latter place a fine Elizabethan house once served as a booking office; at Murrow the M&GN crossed the GN&GEJR on the level. As so often has happened, the long cross-country single line was the most vulnerable to competition. The GER served many of its stations (Wisbech, Lynn, Fakenham, Aylsham, Cromer, Norwich and Yarmouth). Farming produce began to go by road and the lucrative summer passenger traffic began to dwindle for the same reason. Nevertheless, the closure of so many miles of line 'at a stroke' was most disturbing. Track lifting gradually progressed until Breydon viaduct was demolished in December 1962.

Access for walking is easy, for example in the east between Caister and Great Ormesby, the latter station being in private occupation. The chief exceptions are: **Yarmouth Beach** station, now a bus terminal and car park (complete with railway station seat marked 'Gorleston on Sea'); most of the track bed thence to **Potter Heigham** has gone, with a concrete road bridge over the river Thurne in place of the girder railway bridge. From here to **Stalham** the railway has become road A149. There is plenty of good walking until **Gayton Road** is reached, and thence well past **South Lynn** the line has been covered by building sites and road widening. Further west, the going is quite good round **Wisbech**. Between **Bourne** and **Castle Bytham** roads have once again blotted out all traces. **North Walsham** and **Holt** stations have gone, **Massingham** and **Hillington** are privately occupied and **Stalham** is county council offices. Most of the old track between North Walsham and Melton Constable has now been designated a public footpath, called 'Weavers Way'.

Finally do not miss the North Norfolk Railway's preservation scheme between Sheringham and **Holt** with locomotives 61572 (B12) and 7564 (J15) (see Appendix). Those interested in church architecture should not miss those gems of East Anglian art at Walpole St Peter, West Walton, Walsoken and Terrington St Clement.

Train: The visitor to the M&GN will find that he can go by train to Spalding, King's Lynn, Norwich, North Walsham, Yarmouth and Cromer—an excellent selection.

Bus: Services are many: **W. H. Fowler & Sons,** No 336 Peterborough, Wisbech and Lynn, 34a King's Lynn to Gayton Road; Eastern Counties, No 5 Wroxham, Potter Heigham and Yarmouth, 25 and 402 Melton to Sheringham, 29 and 56 Fakenham to Norwich, 25a and 402 Melton to Norwich, 22 Holt to Sheringham, 401 Aylsham to North Walsham, 10 Aylsham to Norwich, 104 and 415 Wisbech to March; many buses run between Hemsby and Yarmouth. Delaine, No 1 Peterborough to Bourne.

Car: Motorists will find roads A17, A148 and A1101 the best.

17. CHURNET VALLEY RAILWAY

North Rode to Leek and Uttoxeter: act 26th June 1846; opened 13th July 1849. Closed: North Rode to Leek, 7th November 1960; Uttoxeter to Leek, 4th January 1965. Length: 23¼ miles.

In 1846 three companies obtained powers to construct lines in Staffordshire—the Potteries, the Harecastle & Sandbach and the Churnet Valley. In 1847 they fused to become the North Staffordshire Railway and it is along the third of the trio that we propose to walk. G. P. Bidder was the engineer and a very good job he made of the line through difficult country. For example, part of the track bed between Froghall and Uttoxeter was laid on a drained canal and the curves had to be eased as far as possible. Tunnels had to be bored just west of Oakamoor and between Cheddleton and Leekbrook.

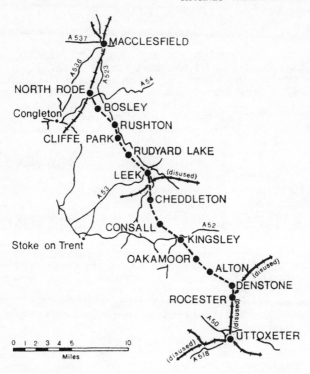

There was also a short tunnel near Leek. The railway was well built but even Bidder's skill could not prevent the serious damage which ensued when the river Churnet burst its banks in 1880 during a period of very heavy rain.

The NSR was noted for the architecture of many of its stations, such as Alton, designed by Pugin, Leek with its imposing colonnade, and the overall excellence of Rushton. Rocester Junction was rebuilt in 1895 as part of a policy of improving the railway's amenities. Some interesting branches deserve brief mention. Near Froghall a tramway of 3ft 6in gauge led off to Caldon Low, dating from 1777. It was a mineral line with cable haulage over inclined planes with certain level sections over which worked an 0-4-0T named *Toad*. The line was closed on 25th March 1920. In 1899 a branch of half a mile ran from Leekbrook to the County Mental Asylum, and it had the distinction of being electrified. It ceased working in 1920. Another offshoot was from Leek to Waterhouses, opened on 1st July 1905, and it is important because it led to a 2ft 6in gauge line which ran thence to Hulme End. This latter line, better known as the Leek & Manifold Light Railway, had opened on 27th June 1904 and was popular with town dwellers as it tapped a beautiful countryside. Unfortunately it was an early victim of road competition, departing this life on 12th March 1934. On the Churnet Valley line Rudyard Lake station was in pretty country and here the railway ran alongside the lake for some distance. It is said that when Kipling's parents were undecided on a name for their son, a relative living in the Churnet Valley suggested 'Rudyard' and the famous poet was named accordingly.

Train services in the early years consisted of four each way on weekdays and two on Sundays. During the last years of the NSR, or 'Knotty' as it was called, as an independent line there were still four weekday trains but on Sundays the four ran between Leek and Macclesfield only. The section north of Leek succumbed first and near the end the Sunday services had disappeared, there being three during the week between Macclesfield and Uttoxeter with two extra on Saturdays, and four in the reverse direction plus one extra Saturday train. The southern half in 1964 ran two trains from Leek to Uttoxeter, and three back, with a trainless Sunday.

The NSR had some pretty little 2-4-0Ts which dealt with the passenger trains on the Churnet Valley line, being known as class B. Sometimes class C 2-4-0 tender engines appeared and goods traffic was entrusted to the hardy class E 0-6-0s. In later years Stanier's class 3 2-6-2Ts did a good deal of the passenger work in conjunction with the larger 2-6-4T type. Freight work was handled by the well-known 4F 0-6-0s.

From **North Rode** the old line can be walked easily past **Bosley**, where the station has gone, to **Rushton** which today possesses the attractive stone-built station, well cared-for as it is owned privately. After **Cliffe Park** one sees the pretty **Rudyard** lake, and the surrounding green hills compensate for the fact that the station has been demolished. The going is quite good but the country is now left behind for the town of **Leek.** Here the station buildings have been demolished and the site has been redeveloped. After Leek the walk can be continued and soon a single-line railway is seen and this extends from **Cheddleton** through **Consall** to **Kingsley & Froghall**. This length of five miles carries mineral traffic only and where there are level crossings, such as at Cheddleton, a notice informs engine crews to *'stop* and open crossing gates'. Cheddleton still has its station building, typical of the 'Knotty' country branch design (plate 21). Kingsley & Froghall buildings have given place to an industrial estate, and the same remarks apply to **Oakamoor,** but the visitor is fully compensated at **Alton.** Here the hills are Staffordshire's best, one being crowned by Alton Castle school, so like Segovia in Spain. The mansion of Alton Towers is nearby, and the railway enthusiast will be delighted to find Pugin's excellent Alton station buildings unharmed (plate 22). Progress can now be made through **Denstone** to **Rocester** where once again industry has blotted out all trace of the line.

Cheddleton station is now the headquarters of the North Staffordshire Railway Museum.

Train: To see the line one can still go by train to Macclesfield, Congleton or Uttoxeter.

Bus: Take the Crosville E15 service of buses from Macclesfield to Bosley; or from Congleton bus K81 to Leek. An alternative is Crosville bus K67 from Biddulph to Leek. From Uttoxeter one can take buses 86A and 86B to Alton and Oakamoor (Potteries Motor Traction Co.). There is also bus 175 from Cheadle to Oakamoor and 176 which goes from Alton to Froghall.

Car: Road A523 will take motorists to the line.

18. BEDFORD TO HITCHIN

Act: 4th August 1853. Opened: 8th May 1857. Length: 16¾ miles. Closed: 31st December 1961.

The Midland Railway was formed in 1844 and was destined to become one of the greatest in the land. Under the vigorous leadership of George Hudson a scheme was proposed in 1846 to build a line to Hitchin and thus become independent of the L&NWR at Rugby. Powers were in fact obtained but the financial stringency after the Mania caused the project to be dropped. Hudson resigned in 1849 but the Midland's dissatisfaction remained owing to the attitude adopted by the L&NWR. The Hitchin scheme was revived in 1852 with suitable encouragement from the owners of iron-ore quarries in Northamptonshire and landed gentry like William Henry Whitbread in Bedfordshire. The outbreak of the Crimean War in 1854 affected the money market and the resulting difficulty in raising capital caused the railway to be made rather more economically than at first planned. Gradients of 1 in 120 and 132 were common, and the line crossed the L&NWR Bedford branch on the level just west of their station, later known as St John's. After Cardington there was a steep climb at 1 in 132 to Warden tunnel which had a length of 880 yards.

Space does not permit more than a passing reference to the later quarrel with the GNR over the congestion on the track between Hitchin and London particularly during the exhibition in London in 1862, and after the accident in a tunnel at Welwyn (North) in 1866. The result was that the Midland built its own line to St Pancras (1868) after which the line to Hitchin was referred to as a branch. It was singled in 1912. In 1857 there were four trains in each direction on weekdays, with two on Sundays, and in 1922 there was the same number of trains during the week, but the Sunday service had gone. This proved to be another 'Beeching' line although British Rail did their best to stimulate travel by introducing diesel trains and 'rail buses' towards the end, running seven trains each way daily, but the Sunday service was never revived. Cardington station was near the village, Southill was not, but Shefford and Henlow were well sited.

The first passenger trains on the Hitchin line were hauled by Kirtley's 2-2-2 engines in green livery, but main-line status was enjoyed for only eleven years. The underline bridges south of Cardington could not support larger engines than class 3 goods, although between Bedford and Cardington it was possible to use class 4 0-6-0s and Stanier class 5 4-6-0s on RAF special trains. As a result, certain difficulties arose with goods trains going south as the class 3 engines would enter Warden tunnel at a walking pace after the long climb from Cardington. If the wind was from the north-west the engine's smoke would follow the train and fill the cab to suffocation point. Driver Rogers of Bedford, who knew the branch well, told the author that in these circumstances he and his mate were compelled to stand outside the engine on the lowest step holding on to a handrail. The locomotive would take the train through on its own, so to speak, and on emerging from the tunnel the crew clambered back into the cab. Fortunately, Warden tunnel was a dry one and the engine 'kept its feet'; had slipping occurred things would have been difficult for the crew.

Two serious accidents occurred on this line. On 20th August 1862 a signalman at Hitchin allowed cattle vans to be shunted on to the Midland track and then forgot about them. A Midland

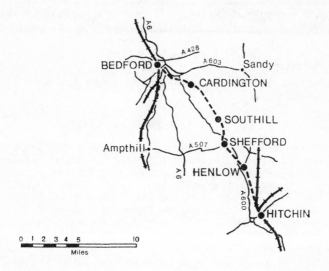

train carrying passengers from Bedford regatta to Hitchin collided with the vans under clear signals, and many people were injured. On 12th March 1875 a Midland train approaching Bedford collided with a L&NWR train on the level crossing previously referred to. A badly placed signal on L&NWR branch to Bletchley permitted their train to cross against the Midland.

The track on the Hitchin line was not lifted until the end of 1964 and in the May of that year a stranger appeared in the shape of Highland Railway 4-6-0 No 103. This was during the making of the film *Those Magnificent Men and their Flying Machines* and No 103 repeatedly climbed the 1 in 132 to Warden tunnel, partly disguised with its train to resemble an express on the Nord Railway of France.

Access to the track bed is not convenient at Bedford but it can be reached at **Cardington** (plate 23) and the remaining stations thence to Hitchin. Warden tunnel is no longer accessible.

It should be noted that Cardington station buildings are used for business purposes, while **Southill** is in private occupation. **Shefford** and **Henlow** have been demolished.

71

Train: From King's Cross to Hitchin, or from St Pancras to Bedford.

Bus: United Counties services 178, Bedford to Cardington; 182, Bedford to Shefford; 181 and 182, Bedford to Henlow and Hitchin.

Car: Roads A600, A6, A603 and A507 will be suitable for motorists.

19. BUXTON TO ROCESTER

Cromford & High Peak Railway (Cromford to Whaley Bridge): act 2nd May 1825; opened July 1831. North Staffordshire Railway (Rocester to Ashbourne): act 22nd July 1848; opened 31st May 1852. London & North Western Railway (Higher Buxton to Ashbourne): various acts; opened to Parsley Hay 1st June 1894, to Ashbourne 4th August 1899. Closed: Hurdlow station, 15th August 1949; Higher Buxton station, 2nd April 1951; remaining stations (except Rocester), 1st November 1954; Rocester, 4th January 1965.

The reader of this chapter who wishes to explore Dove Dale will find that this journey takes him along the route of three lost railways. Going south from Buxton where the LNWR station is still in use as the terminus of the branch from Stockport, the first 3½ miles will be over the line laid down by the LNWR when they began their extension to Ashbourne. Here, at Hindlow, the new branch met the old Cromford & High Peak Railway which was built to link the Cromford Canal with the Peak Forest Canal. The course of the old line is followed as far as Parsley Hay, a distance of 5½ miles, but the gradients and curves were considerably modified as the Cromford & High Peak Railway had included several inclined planes worked by cable.

Nevertheless the improved section included gradients of 1 in 59. From Parsley Hay to Ashbourne (13¼ miles) the hilly country called for many expensive earthworks, and at Ashbourne the LNWR met the NSR or 'Knotty'. Thereafter we walk over the former NSR to Rocester (6¾ miles) where there was a junction with the Churnet Valley line. Ashbourne station is not the original, but dates from 4th August 1890.

The route via Parsley Hay was regarded as a possible alternative for the Euston to Manchester traffic although the mileage was 194 as compared with 183½ via Crewe. However it was never brought up to main-line standards, being largely single-track.

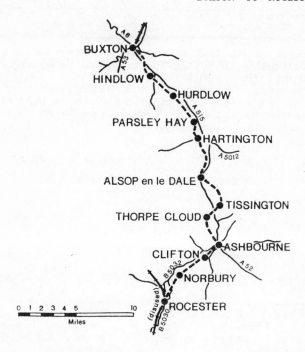

In 1899 there were eight trains between Buxton and Ashbourne and six in the reverse direction on weekdays. By 1920 the number had been reduced to four each way, and immediately before closure there were only three. Sunday services were never run. Freight trains ran until 1964 and the track was lifted the same year. When the demolition train was in progress some of its wagons ran away and demolished three sets of level crossing gates as if in protest at the closure.

It is best to get away from **Rocester** and to follow the track to **Norbury** (plate 24) where the pretty station building is now a private house. At **Clifton** a number of houses are being erected across the track and at **Ashbourne** the passenger station buildings have gone but the goods sheds are in use. The visitor will wish to hurry along the grass-grown trackbed to **Thorpe Cloud** where he will find the weighbridge office and a bridge over the road still in position. Although the station at **Tissington** has

73

gone the scenery here is excellent and the explorer continues the 'Tissington Trail' which will take him along the line on a high embankment with fine views. Tissington village is a gem. One of the best walks to be found is along the old track through **Alsop en le Dale, Hartington,** and **Parsley Hay** to **Hurdlow.** The station buildings are no more but the air is invigorating. It is best to give up at **Hindlow** where a large cement works graces the scene, and a single line for this traffic runs over the viaduct into Buxton. If time permits, see the churches at Ashbourne and Norbury.

Train: Buxton can be reached by train.

Bus: There is a Trent bus from Buxton to Leek, service 28.

Car: Motorists cannot do better than follow road A515.

20. KING'S LYNN TO HUNSTANTON

Opened: 3rd October 1862. Closed: 5th May 1969. Length: 15 miles.

The Great Eastern Railway was constituted on 7th August 1862 and took over the liabilities of the Eastern Counties Railway including the working of branch lines. Two months later the branch from King's Lynn to Hunstanton was opened and, with one exception, this proved to be the only extension for the next four years owing to financial difficulties. Local services amounted to five trains daily to and from Hunstanton, Sundays having one. When in March 1863 the Prince of Wales purchased Sandringham House, the line increased in importance, particularly as regards Wolferton station. On 10th March the train conveying the Prince and his bride Princess Alexandra to Wolferton after their wedding in Westminster Abbey was hauled by Sinclair class W 2-2-2 No 284 painted in a special cream livery. During Johnson's tenure of office as GER locomotive superintendent at Stratford (1866-1873) the celebrated 2-4-0 'Sharpies' worked on the branch, and twenty years later Holden's equally famous T19 2-4-0s handled through trains from London, No 759 being frequently rostered. After 1st July 1870, with the opening of the Tottenham & Hampstead Joint Railway, it was possible to travel from St Pancras to King's Lynn and Hunstanton after a stop at Ely

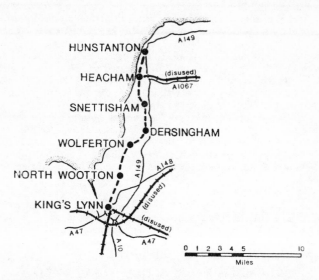

to remarshal the train. It became the custom to allocate one
engine for royal trains, the GER using T19 No 761. In later
years, up to the 1939 war, the L&NER kept two 'Super Clauds'
to work to Wolferton, and these were Nos 8783 and 8787 in
apple-green livery. To keep them in running trim these engines
ran ordinary trains between Cambridge and King's Cross—
say one trip each way per day, and one of them was always
to be found at the head of the 18.55 to Cambridge. On 11th
February 1952 the last sad journey of King George VI took
place, the funeral train being drawn from Wolferton to King's
Lynn by 4-6-0 No 61617 *Ford Castle* (Gresley B17, improved
by Thompson into a B2), and after reversal at Lynn, by BR
standard Pacific No 70000 *Britannia* to London. The final
journey to Windsor from Paddington was behind 4-6-0 No
4082 *Windsor Castle* (actually No 7013 *Bristol Castle* with
altered name and number).

In 1920 near the end of the GER as a separate company,
the local service had been improved to eleven up and twelve
down trains on weekdays, and two each way on Sundays. In
the 1960s, after diesel trains had been introduced, British Rail
maintained an excellent service of eleven down and thirteen up
trains, with six on Sundays. Every effort was made to keep the
line open, including the conversion of the stations to unstaffed

halts and the introduction of 'pay trains'. All the stations were in or near the villages they served. Unfortunately rising costs and the heavy Government investment in roads made a branch of this type most vulnerable, especially under the terms imposed by the Transport Act of 1962, and passenger trains ceased to run in 1969. Goods traffic had disappeared in 1964.

With the exception of some rough ballast near Snettisham the whole line makes good walking with the delightful countryside of west Norfolk close at hand.

Wolferton (plate 26) and **Snettisham** station houses are in private occupation. Snettisham has an interesting church and King's Lynn has much to offer historically and architecturally. **Dersingham** and **Heacham** station buildings are now private dwellings and **Hunstanton's** has been replaced by an amusement park.

Train: to King's Lynn.

Bus: Eastern Counties buses Nos 35, 35a and 35c run from King's Lynn to Hunstanton. No 359 runs between King's Lynn and Wolferton. Through coach Hunstanton to Norwich by service 'T'.

Car: Motorists should use A10 and A149.

21. BALA TO BLAENAU FFESTINIOG

Ffestiniog to Blaenau Ffestiniog (2ft gauge): opened 1868. Bala to Ffestiniog (standard gauge): opened 1st November 1882. Total length 24¾ miles. Closed: 4th January 1960.

Blaenau Ffestiniog was first reached by railway in 1836 when the Ffestiniog Railway finished its line from Portmadoc. The gauge was 1ft 11½in. In 1868 a short line, also of narrow gauge, was opened from Ffestiniog to Blaenau Ffestiniog via Manod, and Samuel Holland, who was a director, wished to extend this small line by means of his Merioneth Railway to meet the Aberystwyth & Welsh Coast Railway near Talsarnau (opened 1863-1869). The Merioneth Railway was not built. The third branch to reach Blaenau Ffestiniog was that of the LNWR which had been extended from Betws y Coed in 1879, and finally the Bala & Ffestiniog was opened in 1882, reaching Blaenau four years later when the narrow gauge line through Manod was widened to 4ft 8½in. The Bala line was worked from the start by the GWR which thereby obtained a share of the slate traffic.

The chief engineering work on the branch is the Cwm Prysor viaduct (plate 27) which blends well with the majestic scenery through which the railway passes. In 1898 the GWR ran five trains each way Monday to Saturday, but as was usual in

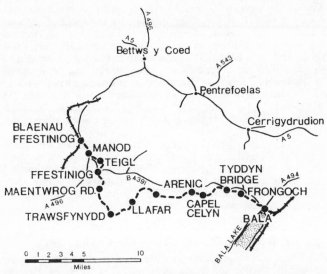

Wales, there was no Sunday service. The number of trains was unaltered in 1922 and for some time thereafter as the GWR was least affected by the Grouping. In order to stimulate passenger traffic seven halts were opened, which with the eight stations gave excellent facilities to the travelling public. Shortly before closure there were three down trains and four up trains (to Bala) with one extra on Tuesdays, Thursdays and Saturdays.

The entire site of **Bala** station is now covered with factories but once in the countryside the track can be picked up very easily with good walking to **Frongoch**. Here the station house is privately occupied and the signal-box shell is in good condition. In selling their stations British Rail have provided many purchasers with dwellings. Conditions are less pleasant at **Arenig** where the Granite Company have expanded all over the site and about a mile of the track bed is now a road. Walking can now be resumed and the country grows wild and lonely near **Cwm Prysor** where the crossing-keeper's cottage is occupied and the gates are in position. Thence, road widening has blotted out the railway, but soon the track is regained high up the side of the hill with fine views and the privilege of walking over the nine-arch viaduct. **Trawsfynydd** station is fortunately in private occupation and well-kept, and the former yard is a coal depot.

The lovely views of Trawsfynydd lake with its rhododendron bushes give way in due course to the ugly buildings of the new atomic power station. From here a single line is retained running right through to the LNWR station at Blaenau Ffestiniog and so to Llandudno Junction to enable the power station to get rid of its atomic waste. The railway can be followed to **Maentwrog Road,** a pretty station privately owned, and so to **Ffestiniog** where the station buildings are *in situ* with the signal-box, brick-built. The line can be followed through **Manod** to **Blaenau Ffestiniog** which lost its beauty when slate-quarrying started.

Formerly Bala was the junction for the Blaenau Ffestiniog and the Dolgellau lines, and the latter survived five years after the closure of the former. Fortunately the track bed of the Dolgellau line now carries the narrow-gauge Bala Lake Railway to Llanuwchllyn. Their motto might well be 'punctuality and politeness'. (See Appendix.)

Train: Happily one can still visit the Bala line by train, going by LMR to Blaenau Ffestiniog and walking south.

Bus: The Crosville buses provide services 93 and 94 from Wrexham to Barmouth via Bala, and No 97 from Bala to Arenig. Bus R36 runs from Dolgellau to Maentwrog and R37 from Tanygrisiau to Ffestiniog. Pwllheli is connected to Blaenau by R27.

Car: B4391 fairly closely follows the old railway.

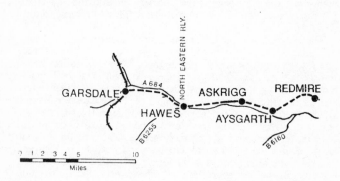

22. NORTHALLERTON TO GARSDALE

Northallerton to Bedale: act 1845; opened 6th July 1848. Bedale to Leyburn: act 1853; opened 19th May 1856. Leyburn to Hawes: act 1869; opened 1st October 1878. Garsdale to Hawes: act 1866; opened 1st October 1878. Closed: Northallerton to Hawes (passenger traffic), 26th April 1954; Hawes to Garsdale (all traffic), 16th March 1959. Length: Northallerton to Hawes, 34 miles (NER); Hawes to Garsdale, 5¾ miles (MR).

It was the great George Hudson who decided on a branch from the main line of the York Newcastle & Berwick Railway at Northallerton to run to Bedale. The Bedale & Leyburn Railway had a separate existence of only three years when it was absorbed by the North Eastern Railway. The latter company in its turn planned the extension across country to Hawes in the west. The line has always been single throughout except for the section Northallerton to Bedale, and today freight trains operate as far as Redmire. From this point to Garsdale the track has been lifted. The whole branch has been included in this chapter because the twenty-two miles still open to goods traffic provide one with an opportunity of seeing what NER branch line stations were like in their more prosperous days. Almost every station is privately occupied and has well-tended flower gardens, and as there is a level crossing at almost every

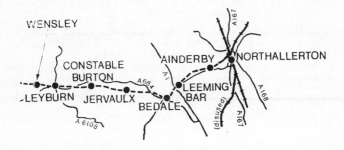

one it has been necessary to install automatic lifting barriers. From Redmire to Garsdale the track bed still forms an excellent pathway for a ramble through lovely Wensleydale. Do not therefore miss seeing **Bedale** (plate 28), **Crakehall, Finghall Lane** and **Spennithorne** stations. The last is most attractive with its Flemish-style gable ends. At **Leyburn,** a passing place, the two platforms and signals look almost untouched by the closure (plate 29). On a clear day one can see Middleham Castle, two miles away, which was the home of the Nevilles, and Wensley should be seen because the village is quite outstanding.

Redmire village is also pretty but the station, now serving the stone quarries, is unattractive. It is here that the delightful walk through the dale begins. As the visitor tramps along the former railway he can look across to Bolton Castle, a most impressive sight. The castle is worth a visit for here Mary, Queen of Scots, was imprisoned for a time. The western wing is in disrepair, but the eastern wing is now a public restaurant and deserves patronage. Nearby, the fourteenth-century chapel must not be missed. At **Aysgarth** the station house is in private occupation while the yard is busy as a coal depot. Aysgarth Force is not far away. After **Askrigg,** where the station is used as offices, the explorer reaches **Hawes** where the station buildings are a visitors' centre. The town is very pleasing, especially the Tuesday market. Beyond Hawes the old track crosses the Widdale beck, a tributary of the Ure, by a fine stone viaduct of five arches, and after this the country becomes wilder with hills on each side rising to 2,000 feet. Walking is quite good to **Garsdale** past Mossdale Head viaduct and tunnel although there are sections with loose ballast. The short section of railway, a quarter of a mile, which connected the Midland to the North Eastern at Hawes was a joint line.

In 1878 the NER ran three trains each way during the week, with an extra one between Leyburn and Northallerton but there was no Sunday train. In 1922 there were four trains in each direction over the whole branch, but still no service on Sundays. Just previous to the withdrawal of passenger trains British Rail provided three each way and on Sundays one train ran from Leyburn to Northallerton and back. In 1973 there were two trainloads of stone departing from Redmire daily, with corresponding empties returning and an occasional coal train.

In NER days passenger trains were usually hauled by the well-known Worsdell 0-4-4Ts (LNE G5), a common visitor being 67312, and sometimes by 0-6-2Ts (LNE N8). Goods traffic was in the capable hands of T2 0-8-0s (LNE Q5). The present stone traffic is easily dealt with by class 31 diesel locomotives.

Train: to Northallerton.

Bus: United Service 78 Northallerton-Leyburn; 72/73 Darlington-Northallerton-Bedale; 147 Ripon-Bedale; 127 Ripon-Leyburn-Hawes; 26 Richmond-Aysgarth-Askrigg-Hawes; Ribble Service 565 Kendal-Sedbergh-Hawes.

Car: Those with cars should take roads A684, A168 and A6108.

23. DARLINGTON TO PENRITH

Darlington & Barnard Castle Railway: act 14th July 1854; opened 8th July 1856. South Durham & Lancashire Union Railway: act 1857; opened, Barnard Castle to Barras, 26th March 1861, Barras to Tebay, 8th August 1861. Eden Valley Railway (Kirkby Stephen to Clifton Junction): act 21st May 1858; opened 7th June 1862. Length: 64¾ miles. Closed: to passenger traffic, 22nd January 1962.

Darlington was joined to Penrith by the enterprise of three separate companies. The Darlington & Barnard Castle Act was unopposed and trains began to run in 1856, but after two years the concern was taken over by the Stockton & Darlington Railway. The South Durham Company also had a short independent existence, being absorbed into the S&DR empire one year after opening. The Eden Valley line planned to run from Clifton Junction, which was on the Lancaster & Carlisle Railway (opened 17th December 1847), to Kirkby Stephen on the South Durham. They amalgamated with the S&DR almost at once, but this proud and profitable line joined the North Eastern in 1863 and thus the Eden Valley soon became part of the great NER. By forming a junction at Kirkby Stephen the Eden Valley line missed serving Brough, which remained the largest town in the area without railway connection. Bradshaw used to insert a special note against the entry for Warcop station—'2¾ miles from Brough'.

The western part of the railway involved the company in great engineering works. Just south of Lartington was the Deepdale viaduct over the beck of that name, and a little south of Barras trains crossed over the deep valley of the river Belah on a viaduct of gigantic proportions. The Belah viaduct was 1,040 feet in length and 196 feet high, and cost £32,000. Both Deepdale and Belah viaducts were of iron construction built to the designs of the celebrated engineer Sir Thomas Bouch. Travelling over the Belah was the nearest thing to flying and

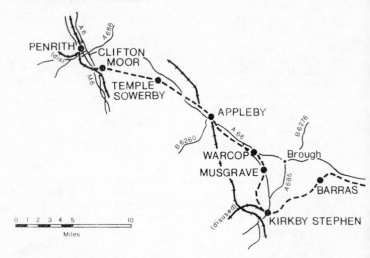

from the ground the columns looked slender, although they did their duty well for 101 years. It is unfortunate that these two structures have disappeared; they were the victims of their own value in scrap metal. Near Temple Sowerby there is a viaduct over the river Eden. Between Bowes and Barras stations lay Stainmore summit where the line reached a height of 1,370 feet above sea level and, as might be expected, the gradients were severe, with a rise to Stainmore at 1 in 67 and another at Barras of 1 in 60.

At the outset there were four trains daily in each direction between Darlington and Kirkby Stephen, with only one train on Sundays and that from Darlington to Barnard Castle and back. On the Kirkby Stephen to Penrith section there were also four trains each way on weekdays, Sunday services being absent. Sixty years later the frequency was unaltered except that on Sundays one train ran from Penrith through to Darlington. Immediately before closure there were three trains in each direction between Penrith and Darlington on weekdays, reduced to one on Sundays. The track was lifted soon after the end of 1962 with the exception of eight miles between Appleby East and Merrygill box at Musgrave. The stone quarries at Merrygill require two or three freight trains each week.

In 1861 two locomotives were supplied by Robert Stephenson & Co to work between Darlington and Kirkby Stephen; they

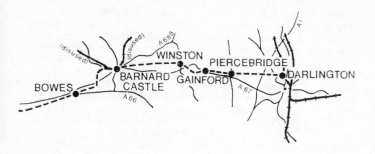

bore the names *Lowther* and *Brougham*. Later the work was performed by the efficient NER C class of 0-6-0 (LNE J21). Driver A. J. Watson, whose daily work took him over this line, had many interesting reminiscences with strong loyalty to the L&NER. He said that the G5 0-4-4T engines were occasionally used on passenger work but normally the C class 0-6-0s were used because of the greater water capacity of a tender. For goods work the P1 0-6-0 (J25) was unexcelled, being able to haul eighteen loaded wagons over Stainmore whereas two LMS class 2 2-6-0s together could manage only fourteen. Of the latter he usually drove 46470 or 46481. When the freight trains became heavier, as they did during the 1939 war, it was necessary to employ T1 0-8-0s (Q5). After the war it was decided that Belah viaduct could support the weight of the superheated T2s (Q6) and accordingly Nos 63355 and 63373 were sent across to Kirkby Stephen shed. There was one double chimney Ivatt 2-6-0, No 43038, which was a poor steamer and he much preferred the BR standard version such as 76047, 76048 and 76051. These were his regular engines, but the first of the three developed the unfortunate habit of losing a mud-hole door while on the move when its entire motive and braking power disappeared in a cloud of steam. Shed 51H also received three BR standard class 2 2-6-0s which he again thought superior to the LMS type and got good work out of Nos

78016/7/8/9. In Eastern Region days, engines used to work right through to Penrith. This is a summary of a conversation with a man who spent his lifetime on engines over this route and in every kind of weather. Readers of Conan Doyle will not fail to note that the author made his enquiries at Musgrave where a Mr Holmes sent him to see driver Watson.

The route is excellent for walking. At **Piercebridge** the station has disappeared and the site is built over. **Gainford** too has gone and St Peter's School is demolished. **Winston** station house is private and the yard is used as a coal depot. You will search in vain for the station at **Barnard Castle,** which was the junction for Bishop Auckland and Middleton, as the Glaxo factory and car park have blotted it out. The old castle here must be visited. **Lartington** station is also privately occupied and is in pretty wooded surroundings, but the environment becomes wilder over Bowes Moor. **Bowes** station buildings have disappeared. There is excellent walking past **Barras** station where the station house is now a residence, but care is needed on the approach to the former Belah viaduct. The stone abutment may be inspected with due respect to the sheer drop into the valley, after which one may pick up the trail on the other side of the river. **Kirkby Stephen** station buildings are used as offices and, soon after, the freight line appears and runs as far as **Appleby East.** Here there is a junction with the West station. There are three trainloads of stone a week hauled by class 37 diesel locomotives. The intermediate stations of **Musgrave** and **Warcop** have their buildings intact, and are occupied privately, but at Appleby East the buildings are used to house the buses of the Ribble company. From Appleby, the walk can be continued through **Temple Sowerby** to **Clifton Junction** in pleasant countryside.

Train: If you go by train choose Darlington, Appleby West or Penrith.

Bus: United Service 75 Darlington-Piercebridge-Gainford-Barnard Castle; 76 Barnard Castle-Middleton; 77 Ingleton-South Cleatlam-Barnard Castle; Ribble Services 620, 621, 622, 623, 624, 625 Kirkby Stephen-Appleby-Penrith; GNE Services Darlington-Barnard Castle-Appleby-Penrith.

Car: Roads A66 and A67 should be taken.

APPENDIX

Preserved railways referred to in the text

Chapter 4. Somerset & Dorset Railway Museum Trust
Headquarters: Washford, Somerset. *Original line:* Somerset & Dorset Joint Railway, opened 1854 to 1890, closed 1966. *Trust formed:* 1971. *Locomotives:* S&DJR 2-8-0 53808; LMS 0-6-0T; several industrial 0-6-0ST by Bagnall HL; Pecket and Avonside. *Plans:* further museum acquisitions.

Chapter 7. Great Central Railway (1976) Ltd
Successors to Main Line Steam Trust. *Headquarters:* Loughborough (GC) station. *Original line:* Great Central Railway, opened 1899, closed 1966-9. *Company formed:* 1976. *First train ran:* 1977. *Length:* 5 miles. *Train services:* weekends all year, Wednesdays May to September. *Locomotives:* N2 4744; B1 1306 and 1264; 0-6-0ST *Robert Nelson;* BR Class 8 71000; BR 2-10-0 92212; GWR 2-8-0T 5224; 4-6-0 6990; SR 4-6-2 34039. *Stations:* Loughborough, Quorn, Rothley. *Plans:* extension to Belgrave.

Chapter 7. Buckinghamshire Railway Centre
Headquarters: Quainton Road Station, Aylesbury. *Original line:* Aylesbury & Buckingham Railway, opened 1868, closed 1936. *Company formed:* 1969. *Locomotives:* Met 0-4-4T L44; LT 0-6-0PT L92; 2-6-2T 41298; Aveling 0-4-0T; 4-6-0 6989; 2-6-0 46447; LSWR 2-4-0WT 0314; GWR 2-8-2T 7200; 0-6-0PT 7715; 4-6-0 6024; LMS 2-6-2T 41313.

Chapter 9. Nene Valley Railway
Supported by the Nene Valley Railway Society. *Headquarters:* Wansford station, Stibbington, Peterborough. *Original line:* Northampton & Peterborough Railway, opened 1845, closed 1957. *Society formed:* 1970. *First train ran:* 1977. *Length:* 6 miles. *Train services:* weekends April-July; Tuesday, Wednesday and Thursday also in July and August; restaurant car. *Locomotives:* Danish 0-6-0T 656; 4-6-2 34081; DB 2-6-2T; Nord Compound 4-6-0; Swedish 2-6-2T and 2-6-4T; 0-6-0ST *Jacks Green;* Class 5 4-6-0 73050; BR 4-6-2 70000; Danish 2-6-4T, ex BR diesel 55016 and 55022. Italian-built wagon restaurant. *Stations:* Yarwell, Wansford, Ferry Meadows, Orton Mere. 60 foot diameter turntable. *Plans:* extension to Peterborough.

Chapter 11. Bluebell Railway
Supported by Preservation Society. *Headquarters:* Sheffield Park station, Uckfield, Sussex. *Original line:* Lewes & East Grinstead Railway, opened 1882, closed 1955 and 1958. *Society formed:* 1959. *First train ran:* 1960. *Length:* 5 miles. *Train services:* winter—weekends; summer—every day. *Locomotives:* U 2-6-0 1618; H0-4-4T 263; BR 2-6-4T 80100; GW 9017; BR 2-10-0 92240; SEC 0-6-0 592; 21C123 *Blackmore Vale;* SEC P tanks;

Adams Radial tank; USA 30064; E4 *Birch Grove;* LBSC Terriers; BR 75027; ex SR 4-6-2 34023 and 34059; 0-6-0 33001; ex BR 2-6-0 78059. *Stations:* Sheffield Park and Horsted Keynes. *Plans:* extend to West Hoathly.

Chapter 15. Colne Valley Railway Company Ltd
Headquarters: Castle Hedingham station, Halstead, Essex. *Original line:* Colne Valley & Halstead Railway, opened 1863, closed 1962. *Company formed:* 1972. *Locomotives:* Hunslet, Vulcan and RSH 0-6-0ST; Avonside and HL 0-4-0Ts. *Stations:* exact replicas of Castle Hedingham and Halstead stations on new site. *Plans:* extension of track and acquisition of rolling stock.

Chapter 15. East Anglian Railway Museum
Headquarters: Chappel station yard, Essex. *Original line:* Stour Valley Railway, opened 1849, closed beyond Sudbury 1967. *Society formed:* 1968. *Locomotives:* Bagnall 0-4-0ST *Jubilee;* RSH 0-6-0ST *Jupiter:* Hunslet 0-6-0ST; Andrew Barclay 0-4-0ST; N7 69621; ex BR 2-6-4T 80151. *Plans:* extension of track and acquisition of rolling stock.

Chapter 16. Midland & Great Northern Joint Railway Society
In conjunction with the North Norfolk Railway. *Headquarters:* Sheringham station, Norfolk. *Original line:* Midland & Great Northern Joint Railway, opened between 1858 and 1894, closed 1959. *Society formed:* 1962 and 1967; North Norfolk Railway 1970. *First train ran:* 1976. *Length:* 4 miles. *Train service:* weekends April to September; also Tuesdays, Wednesdays and Thursdays July to September. *Locomotives:* LNER B12 1572; J15 564; twelve industrial tank engines of 0-4-0 and 0-6-0 design. *Stations:* Sheringham, Weybourne and High Kelling. *Plans:* extension to Holt.

Chapter 17. North Staffordshire Railway Museum
Headquarters: Cheddleton Station, Leek, Staffordshire. Original line opened 1849, closed to passengers 1965. Society formed 1981. Locomotives: BR Standard 2-6-4T No 80136, LMS 4F 0-6-0 No 44422.

Chapter 21. Bala Lake Railway (Rheilffordd Llyn Tegid)
Supported by the Bala Lake Railway Society (Cymdeithas Rheilffordd Llyn Tegid). *Gauge:* 1 foot 11½ inches. *Headquarters:* Llanuwchllyn station, Bala, Gwynedd. *Original line:* Bala and Dolgellau Railway, opened 1868, closed 1965. *Company formed:* 1971. *First train ran:* 1972. *Length:* 4½ miles of superbly maintained narrow-gauge track. *Train services:* weekends spring and autumn; daily Easter to 30th September. *Locomotives:* *Maid Marian* 0-4-0ST (Hunslet); *Holy War* 0-4-0ST Hunslet; *Meirionydd* diesel B-B Severn Lamb 1973, and others. *Stations:* Llanuwchllyn and Bala Lake (Llyn Tegid). *Plans:* extension of ½ mile to Bala town.

INDEX OF PLACES